I WAS A STRANGER AND . . .

I Was a Stranger and...

JOYCE AND MORGAN ILGENFRITZ'S
MINISTRY TO THE
HURTING AND HOMELESS

by

Anthony J. Bachman

CHRISTIAN PUBLICATIONS

Camp Hill, Pennsylvania

Christian Publications
3825 Hartzdale Drive, Camp Hill, PA 17011

The mark of  vibrant faith

ISBN: 0-87509-401-5
LOC Catalog Card Number: 87-72975
© 1988 by Christian Publications
Printed in the United States of America

Scripture quotations are from the HOLY BIBLE: NEW
INTERNATIONAL VERSION. Copyright © 1973, 1978,
1984 by the International Bible Society. Used by permission of Zondervan Bible Publishers.

Drawings by Karl Foster.
Photographs by Mike Saunier.

CONTENTS

I WAS A STRANGER AND . . .

Junko

Angel and Angelina

Lien, Tri and Tam

Morgan and Joyce Ilgenfritz

Beth, Amy, Mark and Shonna Ilgenfritz

nny

Claude

FOREWORD

The Christian home as a redemption center in society is a topic about which I have very strong feelings. I am convinced that gifted individuals can have a profound influence on our culture simply by opening their homes to those who are abandoned, neglected, misused or in need. In fact, I believe there are some people who are so utterly damaged that they will never know God's love apart from the nurturing environment of a Christian family.

Family life in our culture is so disrupted that many children and young adults have no concept of what a healthy family is. Many people have had no exposure to spirituality in any form, and they need to see what it looks like on the most primary level—the Christian family—in order to make an intelligent choice for their own future living.

God has placed in neighborhoods all across the country Christians who have the ability to bring into their own homes and lives many disenfranchised people. These unusual families are discovering that their homes can be redemptive communities as they model, in the most practical, hands-on way, Christ's healing love. Quietly, sometimes with great pain and sometimes with great joy, these families are helping to change society.

My husband, David, and I are watching the process of redemption in the life of a young woman who is now living with us. While watching the daily effect of divine love on this one life, I have cried, prayed, fasted and laughed. And I am more aware than I have ever been in my entire Christian journey of our God's powerful, redemptive ability. There is nothing that quite matches the daily miracles we see taking place in our home.

I strongly recommend that you read the amazing story of Joyce and Morgan Ilgenfritz. Then I challenge you to listen to the calling that the Holy Spirit may be laying on your own heart. This may not be a ministry for all, but it is a ministry of which all must be aware.

KAREN BURTON MAINS

CHAPTER

1

The False Alarm

THE BELL IN THE HALLWAY chimed insistently. It stopped for a moment, then rang again, this time accompanied by loud curses and an angry tirade.

In the kitchen, Joyce hurried to finish her work.

"Where is that nurse?" Joyce heard the elderly man roar from his bed. Although bedridden for a number of years now, Claude Banks still remained an imposing figure, due partly to his lean, 6′ 4″ figure. "Doesn't she hear my bell?" he continued. "What is taking her so long? Joyce, where are you?"

Quickly pouring a cup of steaming coffee for her patient, Joyce headed toward the tornado of invectives. "Here is your coffee, Claude" she said cheerfully.

"Where have you been?" Claude muttered, ignoring both her and the coffee. "You know when my bell rings, you are to come immediately." He paused a moment in his indignation, then continued on. "Where is my medicine? Is it time for my medicine?"

Joyce's cheery smile turned to a frown at these words. "Claude," she said, looking him straight in the eye, "you know that you took your medicine only five minutes ago."

"I did not," he rebutted. "I have been ringing this bell for the last 10 minutes. You could not have given me my dosage."

"Now Claude, I know I gave you that medicine, and I am not giving you more than the doctor prescribed."

Silenced for the moment by her reprimand, Claude thought and then pointed to the trash can by his bed. "Look at this!" he said, pulling out three partially bloodstained tissues. "That shot you gave me was no good. It was a bleeder. You missed the vein, and I need another shot!"

"Sorry, Claude, no more medicine." Joyce then proceeded to take his pulse. In the process she noticed a small cut on his arm. "What is this?" she said. "Is this small cut your so-called bleeder?"

The accusation infuriated Claude, and he immediately launched into another barrage of profanity. Joyce began cleaning the clutter in the room, pretending not to hear Claude's rantings.

Suddenly he stopped. "You may leave immediately," he ordered. "Get out of here. I do not want to see you anymore." Then he stopped talking and watched her cleaning. As she reached to pick up the morning's newspaper, he tried to stop her, but was too slow. Joyce already had the paper in her hand.

"Claude," Joyce said angrily, "Where did you get this?"

There under the newspaper was an unopened bottle of whiskey. For the first time that day, Claude was silent.

"Up to your old tricks again, huh, Claude?" Nothing upset Joyce more than Claude's drinking. She had worked hard to break his addiction. This was, in fact, the reason for his illness. He was an alcoholic, but he was also addicted to Demerol—a drug given to relieve pain after Claude underwent back surgery several years before. That was another reason he needed a nurse: he required a Demerol injection every three hours around the clock.

Joyce grabbed the bottle, hurried to the bathroom and poured its contents down the toilet. Claude's silence changed to cursing.

As Joyce dropped the empty bottle into the trash can, she comforted Claude, "It is getting late. I will bring you your sleeping pills." This brought half a smile to his face.

Leaving the room, Joyce gave a sigh of exhaustion and despair. But she also felt relief. It had been quite a struggle since she and her husband, Morgan, gave up their home of 13 years to move into this 19-room house to care for this sickly man. Not only had it been a strain on Joyce and Morgan, but on their four children as well, who had to adjust to new friends, a new school and a new lifestyle.

Doubts over the validity of such a move often crossed Joyce's mind. Claude was becoming more and more demanding of her, and his unruliness seemed to be getting worse.

"Here are your sleeping pills," Joyce announced as she reentered the room, producing four pills in the palm of her hand.

"Just lay them on the table," Claude responded. "I will take them shortly. I want to drink my coffee first."

"OK," Joyce replied, smiling as she left the

room. Claude had quieted down and was now contentedly sipping his coffee.

Later that evening as Joyce walked by Claude's room, she found her youngest child, Beth, a toddler, at the foot of Claude's bed. "Beth, you naughty girl. Did you crawl out of bed? Say good night to Uncle Claude and get right back in bed," she ordered, taking Beth by the hand and leading her back upstairs.

After making sure that Beth was tucked in, Joyce went back to Claude's room. "Claude, did you take your pills?" she asked, noticing that they were missing.

"No," he responded.

"Are you sure?"

"Of course I am sure!" he replied rather disgustedly.

Panic swept over Joyce as she dashed to Beth's room. She swooped the child up in her arms and rushed downstairs.

"Morgan, I think Beth just took four of Claude's sleeping pills!"

They ran to the car and drove the six blocks to the hospital. Beth received a series of tests and had her stomach pumped only to have the results turn out negative. Their fear suddenly gave way to disgust and anger. Claude had tricked them again.

Upon their return home, they found Claude sleeping like a baby. Returning Beth to her bed, Joyce retired to her favorite secluded spot in the house, the stairs from the kitchen to the family room in the basement. Often after Claude's verbal abuses and acts of deception, Joyce would retreat to this haven of comfort to be alone and cry. Tonight was no exception.

Still seething in anger, Joyce vented her frustrations about Claude. *How could he do that?* she thought to herself as the tears streamed down her face. *Anything for more drugs. Poor Beth!*

Frustration led to doubt. *I cannot believe Morgan and I sold our house for this gruesome place where everything has turned into a nightmare. To think that we promised to take care of that old man until he dies. Are we going to be stuck with him forever? Did we make the wrong decision?*

After several minutes of these thoughts, the despair seemed to fade, and Joyce began to pray. "Jesus, forgive me for my doubts. I know you have given me the verse in Jeremiah 33:3 to claim, 'Call unto me, and I will answer thee, and shew thee great and mighty things, which thou knowest not' (KJV). I know You have a plan for Claude's life, and I know You have a plan for my life. That is why You brought me and my family here."

Concluding her prayer, Joyce began to think. God *did* have a plan for her life. As she looked back over events from her past, she could see that He had directed every step of the way. Each event in her life was significant; each had led to this point. But little did she know what exciting things God had in store for the future.

CHAPTER

2

A Nursing Career

Since she was five years old, Joyce had wanted to be a nurse. She grew up with that wish, but had it not been for her father's stern discipline and meeting Morgan, her husband, the dream could never have been realized.

Thinking of her husband and God's goodness brought back fond memories. Sitting on the steps, Joyce remembered the first time she saw Morgan.

Joyce Miller and Morgan Ilgenfritz met as children. She was five, and he was eight. Morgan lived with his grandparents, who had sold their home to Joyce's parents. When Morgan returned to the neighborhood to visit relatives, he would play with the Miller children. Even at that young age, Morgan fascinated Joyce, not only with his boyish good looks, but with his wit and charm—and his artificial thumb with which he pulled stingers out of bees!

Twelve years later, Joyce, now an energetic young woman, was working at Murphy's Five and Dime store as a clerk, when Morgan's aunt came in. Joyce introduced herself and asked if she had a nephew called Morgie.

"Yes, I do," she replied. "How do you know him?"

8

"I remember when he used to pull stingers out of bumblebees with his artificial thumb," she confessed, half blushing. "What is he doing now?"

"He is in the Navy," Morgan's aunt boasted proudly.

This shocked Joyce, because she still pictured him as an eight-year-old. "The next time you see him, will you tell him that Joyce Miller asked about him?"

Joyce never expected her request to be granted so quickly. That weekend Morgan came home on leave from Philadelphia. When he heard about Joyce's interest, he decided to pay her a visit. As he climbed the porch stairs up to the Miller house, he overheard loud voices. Joyce and her dad were in the heat of battle. Another young man and Joyce had exchanged school rings at a party. When her dad noticed the ring hanging around her neck, he quickly ordered her to return it. Joyce refused to do so and ran up to her room in tears.

Morgan hesitantly knocked on the door. "Hello, I am Morgan Ilgenfritz. Is Joyce home?" he asked a surprised Mr. Miller.

"Morgan Ilgenfritz?" Mr. Miller paused to think for a second. "Oh yes! Come in and have a seat. Joyce is upstairs. I will let her know you are here."

Mr. Miller went to the kitchen, grabbed a moist cloth and ascended the stairs. "Joyce," he said, "wash your face and get downstairs. There is a young man waiting for you!"

"Daddy, I don't want to go!" she pleaded through her closed door.

Mr. Miller ended the conversation, "I will see you downstairs shortly."

Submitting to his authority, Joyce washed her tear-stained face and slowly headed down the stairs to meet the mystery man.

"Hello, I am Morgan," he said as soon as he spotted Joyce. "My aunt told me that you asked about me."

Joyce stood speechless, gazing at his hand quickly to see if he still had his artificial thumb. As they began to talk, Joyce suddenly realized that the chain holding the disputed ring still hung around her neck in full view. *Morgan might see it*, she thought. Cunningly she slipped it into her blouse, not wanting Morgan to think she was "taken." The rest of the visit proved enjoyable.

The following weekend, Joyce and her girlfriend were walking down the street when Morgan pulled up in his father's Plymouth. "Hello girls! Would you like a ride?" he asked.

Surprised by his offer, Joyce responded, "What are you doing here?"

"This is my last leave of absence before going to Cuba. I wanted to ask you to write to me."

"Sure, I would love to write," Joyce replied in a daze.

The two corresponded for several months. As Morgan's Christmas leave approached, Joyce became so excited that she broke out in hives.

Yes, those were good memories, but Joyce remembered other events, events that had not been as pleasant. Numerous confrontations with her father unknowingly affected her decision to become a nurse.

Joyce's childhood desire to be a nurse, sparked

by a toy nursing kit she had received for Christmas, met with resistance from her father. He tried to discourage her not because he did not want her to be a nurse but because of the family financial situation. "Joyce, I want to tell you something," he said one day. "We have nine children, and I don't have the money you'll need to go to nursing school. If I sent you to nursing school, I would have to agree to send your brothers and sisters to college also. We just don't have the money for that."

"But Daddy," she answered, looking into his eyes, "I want to be a nurse so badly that we will just have to find a way!"

Just two weeks later, Joyce was overjoyed when she learned of an offer from the Professional Business Woman's Club. They were going to provide her an interest-free loan to attend nursing school. Her English teacher, who was a member of the club, knew of her situation and convinced the group to supply the loan.

But the nursing dream almost vanished that summer. With Morgan at sea and Joyce almost ready to graduate from high school, her thoughts turned to taking a summer job at the seashore. The day after her graduation, Joyce and three friends headed to Wildwood, New Jersey, to work at a Kohr Brothers' frozen custard stand.

Her father had consented, because Joyce agreed to send home the money she would earn for her schooling. Even though she was only going to make $35 a week, Joyce promised to send home $30 out of each paycheck—a small price to pay, thought Joyce, for being able to live at the shore for the summer.

The first week Joyce sent home the $30. The second week it dropped to $25. By the third week, the amount had dwindled to $20. The fourth week she called home to tell her father she saw a nice pair of sandals and had purchased them. Nothing came home that week.

Finally her father called her on the telephone, "Joyce, I've been thinking. I have a bad feeling about your working down there. I wonder, have you forgotten about nursing?"

"No, Daddy, I haven't. What makes you think that?"

"Each week we are getting less and less for your savings for nursing school. I feel that you should quit your job and come home."

"Daddy, I will not!" Joyce said almost in tears.

"I insist on it!"

In a fit of anger, Joyce hung up the phone and stormed off to work. Her anger soon subsided with the business of the evening, but a real shock came at midnight when Joyce found her father standing by her side.

"What are you doing here, Daddy?"

"I came to take you home," he replied.

"You cannot do this!" she insisted.

"That is what you think," he flashed back as he walked over to the manager and notified him of her departure as soon as her responsibilities for the night were met.

Finally at 2:00 A.M., he grabbed her by the hand and escorted her down the boardwalk to his car. Joyce cried all the way home.

"Go ahead and cry if that makes you feel better," he consoled, "but you *are* coming home."

How grateful Joyce is today that her father took

such a bold stand. If she had stayed at the shore for the entire summer, she would never have entered nursing school. Her correspondence with Morgan had also dwindled, and she almost forgot about him.

Just before Joyce left for nursing school that fall, Morgan came home. Not wanting to interfere with her plans for nursing school, he decided to move to North Carolina. The night he left, Joyce committed herself to a nursing career.

After that, Morgan and Joyce stopped seeing each other. Then, out of the blue, Morgan called from Norfolk one night and proposed to Joyce. And Joyce accepted!

More than half of the girls in Joyce's nursing class never graduated. Some got married; others simply left. But Morgan kept encouraging Joyce, never asking her to quit so they could marry. In spite of his encouragement, though, she almost quit three times because of discouragement— once even to the point of having her bags packed—but Morgan always insisted she continue.

Nursing would not have been a reality if it had not been for Joyce's father and Morgan. Now, as she sat reminiscing on the steps, she knew that God, too, had nursing as part of His plan for her life.

CHAPTER

Patience for a Patient

Back in the present, Joyce sighed to herself. The day's events came back to her, and she started thinking again about Claude. Soon her thoughts drifted back to the time when she first met him.

It all began one Sunday in 1965 when a lady at church asked Joyce to relieve her for a week as private-duty nurse for an elderly man. Since it would not interfere with her regular job, she agreed. In the morning, she would stop at his house, check on him, give him his medicine and let the dog out. In the evening, she would prepare him for bed, lock the house and put the dog in the garage.

After the second day, she began to experience an uneasiness about the situation. At night, she found herself hurrying to her car, frightened by the darkness created by overgrown foliage around the house. Because of Claude's desire for seclusion and his neglect of the yard, the house could barely be seen from the road.

Ironically, though, this house had once been the social center of the neighborhood, with as many as three open bars serving at one time dur-

14

ing parties. Claude himself seemed to have everything going for him. He owned his own construction company, lived in this gorgeous house and was married to a beautiful woman 18 years his junior. Then his wife died—something he had never anticipated and something he could not accept. From then on, he chose to live as a recluse. He turned to drinking and drugs for solace.

Soon, Joyce found herself regretting her decision to look after Claude. He behaved mysteriously and made her edgy. He seemed to know her every move, even during her absence from the bedroom.

"I hate that job," she told Morgan one night. "I don't ever want to go back."

"In all the time you have been a nurse," he replied, "I have never seen you act like this. What is wrong?"

"I don't know. I just have bad feelings about the whole situation."

Soon the week was over, and Joyce felt relieved. A short time later, however, she was asked to care for him again. Eventually, caring for Claude became a regular obligation for Joyce. Because of Claude's strange and demanding personality, nurses refused to work for him. In the end, Joyce was the only nurse Claude could get. Part of her reason for staying was because she recognized that loneliness was Claude's biggest problem. She saw beneath his tough exterior to the hurting man within. More than anything, he wanted attention; he wanted someone to care about him and that was what kept Joyce coming back.

As part of his ploy for attention, Claude constantly played the invalid. As soon as Joyce left for the night, though, he would get out of bed and search for a bottle of alcohol.

After Joyce had worked with Claude for a number of weeks, she and Morgan began receiving phone calls about him during the night. He would call the operator, giving her the Ilgenfritz telephone number before passing out from intoxication. The operator then called Joyce and Morgan, relaying his pleas. Before going to work in the morning, they would both travel to Claude's house to check on him. They usually found him stretched out on the floor, unable to return to bed.

After four or five such calls, Morgan's patience began to grow thin. Then came the 4:00 A.M. call. The telephone operator told them Claude sounded different that night. She suggested they investigate immediately. Rushing to his house, they found Claude face down on the floor, unconscious in a pool of vomit and blood. He had apparently struck his head on the window sill after passing out.

Bewildered, Joyce looked at Morgan. "What are we going to do?" she asked.

"There is only one thing we can do," Morgan decided. "We must take him home with us. At least in that way he will not be able to get anything to drink."

Morgan lifted Claude by his shoulders while Joyce held his feet, and the two of them carried him downstairs, through the doorway and placed him in the back seat of the car. Back at their house, they carried him inside, cleaned him up and placed him in bed.

When he recovered about two o'clock the next

afternoon, he asked in a surprised voice, "What am I doing here? Get me out of here!" He ranted and raved all day about wanting a drink, but Joyce refused.

Claude was under a physician's care and was seen two to three times per week. When the doctor found out about Claude's latest episode, he ordered him to either stay at the Ilgenfritz house or go to a nursing home. The doctor would not allow Claude to return home. Claude refused to go a nursing home, saying that if he went there, he would die. So finally, an arrangement was made where Claude would stay at the Ilgenfritzes.

For the first two weeks, they restrained Claude in bed, and he agonized through withdrawal. As he showed signs of improvement, Joyce and Morgan agreed to let him return home on weekends, as long as he would stay with them during the week. This proved to be a mistake. On those weekends he paid someone to bring him alcohol and started drinking again. Once Joyce and Morgan discovered this, they canceled his weekend visits home. He now stayed with the Ilgenfritz family seven days a week. His stay at their house lasted for over a year.

CHAPTER
4

White and Clean

MORE THAN THE UPHEAVAL Claude's presence caused in the Ilgenfritz household, his stay had a personal effect on Joyce. She wanted to be able to offer him something real, something life changing, but she felt an emptiness in her own life and knew there was nothing she could give Claude. Remembering this time, Joyce thought about how she had come to question her relationship with God and her own purpose for existence.

In 1968, when Claude moved in, Joyce and Morgan owned a nice house, fully furnished. Both of them had good paying jobs. They had a growing family. Joyce was active in church as a Sunday school teacher and head of the women's organization, but she felt as though she was playing a role. On the outside, she appeared religious; on the inside, she knew something was lacking.

One day Joyce heard that Rex Humbard, well-known television evangelist, was coming to town for a crusade. A strange desire to hear him speak suddenly came over her.

Morgan, on crutches at the time from a knee injury, did not share her enthusiasm when she told him about Rex Humbard. At first he refused to go to the meetings with Joyce, but in the end he finally consented in spite of the frigid February weather.

During his message, Humbard asked an intriguing question. "How would you like to have the wings of a dove and be able to soar above it all?" To Joyce, that sounded inviting.

"Would you like to fly away?" he continued. Joyce knew she wanted to get above her problems.

At the conclusion of his message, Humbard extended an invitation to those who wanted to accept Jesus as their Savior. A number responded to his call. After this, he extended a second invitation and then a third, as more and more people responded. About to close the meeting, he said, "I am going to give only one more invitation. I feel that there is one more person out there who is really struggling and who wants to accept Jesus Christ." Joyce knew that she was that person.

She squirmed in her seat. What would Morgan think? What would those people who knew her as a friend, a Sunday school teacher and head of the church's women's organization think? Then, she did not care anymore. She jumped to her feet and ran down the aisle.

After a short time, Humbard began to talk to those who had come forward, explaining what had happened to them. He held a plain sheet of white paper up before them. "This looks like your new life in Jesus Christ," he explained, "white and clean! This is what happened when you accepted Jesus into your hearts and were born again."

Joyce recalled a Scripture verse in Second Corinthians, "Therefore, if anyone is in Christ, he is a new creation; the old has gone, the new has come!" (5:17). Joyce felt a peace come over her—and at the same time, she felt uplifted in her spirit. She truly felt like "a new creation" and, for the first time, felt that her life had purpose. Joyce also sensed that she had entered a new phase of her life.

Morgan, though, did not share her new-found enthusiasm for spiritual things. In fact, the change that came over Joyce upset him, and he grew to resent it. Morgan had always been a moral person and had attended church on a somewhat regular basis. Many years before, he had even promised to serve God.

It had been at a time when Morgan came down with pneumonia. Right after they were married, Morgan felt it was necessary for him to work three jobs—not because he needed to, but because he had the desire to secure things for his family. He also had the vision of becoming a self-made man.

But the strain on his body caught up with him, and he caught pleurisy pneumonia. This in turn, reduced his resistance to other illnesses.

One morning while shaving, he noticed his vision blurring. After it happened again the next morning, Morgan called Joyce and told her about it. She advised him to see a doctor immediately.

The doctor examined Morgan but did not really uncover the problem. He gave Morgan a prescription and sent him home.

A short time later, though, Morgan began to experience a creeping darkness in his right eye. Back to the doctor again, the problem was now diagnosed as a detached retina. An appointment was made at Johns Hopkins Hospital in Baltimore, Maryland, where more tests and medicine were administered. The doctor here seemed to feel that the mysterious illness was caused by a virus Morgan had contracted during his tour of duty in Korea—a virus that had remained with him until now. When his body's defenses became depleted, the virus had emerged. Being only the second such case ever treated at Johns Hopkins, the prognosis was not promising. In the other case, the patient lost his eye. Morgan was told that they thought they could stop the infection by an operation, but that he might retain only two percent of his vision in that eye.

Deciding that two percent was better than nothing, Morgan agreed to the operation. The procedure was set for a few days later—it just happened to be Christmas time—and Joyce and Morgan returned home to wait for the date. In the meantime, they made arrangements to celebrate an early Christmas with the children.

That Christmas season was a bleak one for Morgan. After the operation, he lay for 11 straight days in darkness, not knowing his fate. During this time, he often talked with his roommate who professed to be a Christian. Somehow, though, his concept of and commitment to God differed from Morgan's. This man felt that God was not only real, but that He was someone whom man could know and talk to. He told Morgan that he felt His presence right in the hospital room with them.

In the solitude of darkness, Morgan began to pray. "God, if You help me out of this situation, I will do Your will."

Part of Morgan's prayer was answered soon after he was released from the hospital. He had used up all of his sick leave, and the bills were piling up. Two of his co-workers presented him with a check from a donation given by his fellow workers.

After the doctor removed his patches, the earlier prediction proved valid; only two percent of his vision remained in his right eye. Morgan now realized that God had answered the other part of his prayer. Though he had lost most of the sight in his right eye, he could still see out of the left one, and he thanked God for that.

Now, years later, Joyce's change reminded him of this promise he had made to God, and he somehow could not escape thinking about it.

CHAPTER
5

The Deal

DURING THE YEAR of Claude's residence at the Ilgenfritz home, Joyce began to notice some changes in his attitudes and actions. For the first time, he began to feel like he was part of a family.

One day he surprised Joyce with a comment: "You know, I would like to have a nurse and her family move into my house with me."

"That is an excellent idea," Joyce agreed. Inwardly, she sighed with relief. Maybe, now, she and Morgan would be free from the burden of caring for Claude.

After a short pause, Claude added, "It sure would be nice having a man around the house to take care of the yard."

"Claude, that would be the best thing you could do," Joyce responded.

The discussion ended, and Joyce thought little more of it. A short while later, however, Claude requested that Joyce and Morgan come to his room. "I have something important to discuss with the two of you," he said.

As they entered his room, Claude started speaking in his usual complaining way. "This is ridiculous! You are expecting another baby, and I am taking up its room. Here, I can stand in the living room and hear everything throughout the

23

rest of the house. At least in my big house I could have my own quiet bedroom and private bathroom."

He paused, gave a quick glance at his listeners, then continued. "How about considering moving into my house?"

Both Joyce and Morgan were taken aback. Move into Claude's house? Impossible. Joyce was the first to respond. "Claude, we could never move away from here. This is our home."

"Come now, I insist. Just think about it," he countered.

At first Joyce refused to even consider it. She loved her home and had no desire to leave it. She and Morgan had lived in their cozy Cape Cod house for nearly 13 years. Morgan had worked constantly on it, building additional bedrooms and an entire upstairs. When the work was completed, they had five bedrooms, and the house had become an integral part of their lives. Their roots were there. Their children had grown up there. They felt that they would live out their lives there. Besides, all Joyce's memories of Claude's house were negative.

Even after much thinking and discussing—and praying by Joyce—neither were inclined to move into Claude's house. Still, they felt they should continue to care for him, so they approached Claude with an alternate plan.

"Claude, we really feel that we cannot move into your house," Morgan began, "but what would you think if we both were to sell our present houses and build a new one with a little house adjoining it for you?"

Claude agreed to the proposition, hired an architect and purchased three lots. Then something incredible happened. After negotiating with five successive buyers, each deal fell through for one reason or another. On the day the fifth buyer withdrew, Joyce and Morgan began to give up the idea. It just was not working out.

One day while Joyce was reading her Bible, the thought suddenly came to her: *What if God was not allowing the house to be sold? Could He be trying to tell me something?*

Joyce relayed these thoughts to Morgan, and although he had not yet committed his life to Christ, he agreed that this could be possible. For the first time, they seriously discussed the possibility of moving into Claude's house. Just a month earlier, Claude had allowed Shonna, their oldest daughter, to hold a birthday party in his recreation room. Without any doubt, the family could use all the space Claude's house had to offer. On the other hand, though, Joyce pictured Claude's being cranky any time the children touched anything in his house.

The next day they presented all their questions to Claude.

"Look," he replied, "if you move there, the house is yours except for my bedroom and bathroom. I do not care what the children do. They can write on the walls as far as I am concerned.

"I'll tell you what," he continued, "if you place your house on the market, sell it and pay off your existing mortgage, I will sell you my house for the balance. I have only one other stipulation. I would want you to take care of me for the rest of my life."

Joyce and Morgan agreed to think about the new proposal.

During this time, Joyce was continually growing in her faith, cultivating her personal relationship with Jesus. While wrestling with the question of moving to Claude's house, she constantly
sought the Lord's will. Eventually the answer became clear: Claude would never accept Jesus as
his personal Savior unless they moved into his
house. Joyce then told Morgan that she would
agree to the move.

The Ilgenfritz house sold quickly. But they now
faced a rather unique problem: two totally furnished homes. Should they discard Claude's
beautiful furniture or sell their new furniture and
appliances?

One night while in bed, Joyce felt the Lord
again plainly speaking to her, "Joyce, I want you
to give everything away; do not sell anything!"
Joyce knew she had to be obedient. And she
knew just who to give it to—her eight brothers
and sisters, many of whom were just setting up
their own households. Giving actually proved to
be fun! Even the custom-made drapes fit Joyce's
brother's windows perfectly. Everyone seemed to
get just what he or she needed.

This step of faith was not simple. After 13
years, Joyce had become attached to the things
she had worked so hard to attain. Joyce remembered the struggle after they moved. Because it
took several months for the closings, she would
often return to her house and sit on the floor in
the living room, reminiscing. This little house,
this beautiful living room was all she had ever
dreamed about.

"Lord," she cried, "I hope we did not make the
wrong choice!"

CHAPTER

Satan at Work

JOYCE AND MORGAN BOTH found the adjustment to a new home difficult. Claude and the Ilgenfritz family came from different backgrounds with different lifestyles. Although the Ilgenfritzes were used to Claude's manner, something new happened once they were situated in his house.

Claude had been accustomed to an affluent life, and he tried to impose his social values on his "new" family. He wanted Joyce and Morgan to join the country club and send their children to the exclusive private school in town. Joyce became concerned about how all of this would affect her family—Morgan especially. She still prayed for his complete surrender to Christ, and while she had seen a gradual change in his attitude about spiritual things, she knew his heart was not right with God. Unknown to Joyce, Claude secretly felt that if he got them involved in these things, Joyce would quit this "Jesus" stuff.

The first couple of months tried their patience. Not only did the children miss their old friends, but Joyce missed talking to her neighbors while hanging out the wash to dry on Mondays. She quickly realized, though, that God was giving her extra time to spend with Him. Her desire to read her Bible and spend time in prayer increased. Her spiritual life did the opposite of what Claude hoped for: it blossomed.

Unfortunately, as Joyce's faith increased, so did Claude's resistance toward hearing the gospel message. Before the move, Claude listened intently when Joyce talked about Jesus, but here, in his own house, he hardened his heart toward it, making life for Joyce even more difficult.

One day Claude ordered Joyce to cook flounder for supper. After he gave her instructions on how to prepare it, Joyce went to the store and bought the necessary ingredients. As she proudly presented her dish to Claude in his room, she received a barrage of profanity and was ordered to leave immediately—flounder in hand. Then she noticed the glassy look in his eyes. Claude had started to drink again. During her absence, he had phoned a cab company which purchased a fifth of whiskey and delivered it to Claude. He drank the whole fifth before Joyce returned.

Joyce left the room in tears. That night was when she found her stairway "retreat." Once there, she began to pray, "Jesus, I was sure You wanted us here and that Claude would accept You as his Savior once we moved. That was the whole reason for our moving here. Have I been deceived?" Indulging in self-pity, she continued to remind Jesus how they had sold their home, given away their possessions and their lives, and now they were stuck with this man.

Claude's demands and irritability steadily increased. Morgan had wired the doorbell chimes in the living room to a push button in Claude's room. He seemed to buzz the chimes constantly and demanded an inordinate amount of Joyce's time.

While the new life at Claude's house served to draw Joyce closer to the Lord, it seemed to have the opposite effect on Morgan. She sensed him slowly slipping away from her and from spiritual things. Before their move, Joyce had found that Morgan was becoming more open to discussing spiritual things, but now it was different. Morgan did not want to hear about Christ. Claude could not wait until Morgan came home so he could offer him a beer. At first Morgan refused to drink with him, but then one day he accepted Claude's offer—a small truimph for Claude!

Every day, Claude would invite Morgan to his room after he arrived home from work, and they would talk about the house and business and sip beer together. Soon, Morgan not only drank with Claude, but carried a can of beer with him as he mowed the lawn and performed other household chores. Eventually, he even brought one to the supper table.

Soon, Joyce could take it no longer. Nearing the point of a nervous breakdown, she visited her doctor. "Joyce, do you feel like you are constantly tired out?" he asked.

"Yes," she sighed.

"I think you are depressed," he finally said. "I am going to give you some tranquilizers. I want you to take these for two weeks and then come back to see me."

Joyce agreed to the recommendation, confident that he would discontinue their use or decrease the dosage after the two weeks. When she returned to his office, she was shocked to learn that he wanted her to continue with an even stronger dosage. That snapped her back into reality and out of her depression. She remembered her struggles with diet pills during her nurse's training. Addiction to them could be easy.

She also remembered hearing a former drug addict from Teen Challenge describe his deliverance from drugs. He claimed that many women were addicts—hooked on diet pills and tranquilizers—and did not even know it. If Jesus had delivered him, Joyce believed He could deliver her. And He did.

Suddenly Joyce understood what was happening. Satan was trying to undermine the situation in any way he could. He had used all the tricks that had succeeded in destroying Claude. He tried to get the Ilgenfritz family into the social trap, tried to get Morgan diverted to drinking and away from spiritual things and nearly drove Joyce into the deadly trap of drugs.

After all these trials, though, hope finally came. One day their oldest daughter, Shonna, came to Joyce and said she was worried about her father's drinking. When Joyce relayed this to Morgan, it seemed to cut to his heart, but he did not stop drinking. Soon after this, they went to a party sponsored by Morgan's hunting club where alcohol was served. He became so intoxicated that he could hardly drive home.

The next day, while Morgan was at work, Joyce poured out her heart to God. At that same exact time, Morgan was driving out to a job. Thoughts of the night before and how the drinking was beginning to take control of his life ran through his head, and he vowed then and there, never to drink again. When he came home that evening and told Joyce and they realized it had occurred at the same time she was praying, they could not help but rejoice.

From that time, Joyce noticed a change in Morgan's openness to spiritual things. Joyce had started attending a new church—the York Christian and Missionary Alliance Church—and Morgan began going with her. He found the people different there and developed a special friendship with the pastor. One Easter morning, the family attended a Family Life Conference that had been recommended by the York Christian School (where the Ilgenfritz children now attended school). The children wanted the family to go, but Morgan was not interested. Finally, the children convinced him. The message that morning was particularly challenging, and when the altar call was given, Morgan went forward and gave himself completely to God.

It was about this same time that Joyce also received the promise concerning Claude's salvation. One night, while she lay awake praying to God, a Scripture verse, Jeremiah 33:3, came to her: "Call unto me, and I will answer thee, and shew thee great and mighty things, which thou knowest not" (KJV). That verse convinced Joyce that Claude would some day know Jesus personally.

CHAPTER

7

From Timidity to Boldness

ALTHOUGH JOYCE FELT God working in her life, and sensed that she was growing in her walk with Him, she did not feel always confident in dealing with daily problems—especially the confrontations with Claude. Something seemed to be missing in her spiritual life, and despite her desire to be loving to Claude, she just could not always have victory after one of his outbursts.

As part of her growing desire to be a witness to people, Joyce volunteered to participate in an evangelism course for counselors for the showing of the Billy Graham film, *Time to Run*. During the film's first showing, Joyce stayed in the rear of the theater, petrified.

Feeling no boldness or power in her life to witness, Joyce prayed, "Jesus, what do I lack?" Immediately a verse in Ephesians popped into her head. "Do not get drunk on wine, . . . Instead, be filled with the Spirit" (5:18).

As she stood in the rear of the theater, she noticed another counselor named Mike. She saw how he readily made himself available to those needing help, boldly witnessing to them about Christ.

During the next showing, he approached Joyce with a big smile, introducing himself. As they conversed, Joyce confessed her lack of power and effectiveness in witnessing. He lovingly smiled at her. "What you need is the power of the Holy Spirit. Would you like to pray and ask God to fill you with His Holy Spirit?"

"Oh yes!" Joyce said.

"Tonight, during the last feature," he instructed, "I will get some of the other counselors, and we will pray for you."

So, during that showing of the film, the group assembled, but they did not know where they should go to pray. Noticing a door that was marked "Rooftop," Mike suggested they go up there and pray. The idea sounded crazy, but somehow appropriate, and the group headed up the stairs.

Unknown to the little prayer group, a police officer spotted their movement on the roof and contacted the theater manager. The manager, of course, had not been advised of the "prayer meeting" and told the officer to investigate. Suddenly the group found themselves bathed in bright spotlight.

"What are you doing up there?" demanded the policeman.

"We're, uh, praying," Mike blurted out.

"Well, . . . would you please pray somewhere else?" the officer requested.

Somewhat embarrassed, the group immediately got up from their knees and headed back down the stairs, giggling as they went. Needless to say, that broke up the prayer meeting. Joyce did not feel any different but remained confident that the Lord would answer prayer.

At four o'clock the next morning, Joyce awoke with a strong urge to be alone with the Lord. She tiptoed downstairs, knelt by a chair and suddenly experienced a flow of praise coming from her lips. Stopping momentarily, she opened her Bible to the Gospel of John and read from the 16th chapter.

> Unless I go away, the Counselor will not come to you; but if I go, I will send him to you. . . . Ask and you shall receive, and your joy will be complete (John 16:7b, 24b).

She then read from the second chapter of the Book of Acts.

> Suddenly a sound like the blowing of a violent wind came from heaven and filled the whole house where they were sitting. They saw what seemed to be tongues of fire that separated and came to rest on each of them. All of them were filled with the Holy Spirit (Acts 2:2–4a).

Again, the tidal wave of praise flowed, as she felt her inmost being filled with the presence of the Holy Spirit.

The next night at the theater, Mike came up to her. Noticing her new radiance, he knew what had happened. The days of hesitating in the rear of the theater were gone. She now felt an urgency to pray with anyone who wanted to know how to receive eternal life.

She also experienced a new confidence in dealing with the daily confrontations with Claude

and witnessing to him. But more than that, she
finally felt that she could love Claude as Jesus
would love him. The Lord had given her a new
kind love and power to serve Claude and to per-
servere.

CHAPTER

Love through a Child's Eyes

DESPITE CLAUDE'S NASTY disposition and the fact that he had a reputation for disliking children, a special relationship developed between him and Joyce and Morgan's children. It was actually the Ilgenfritz children who made Claude a part of the family.

Claude's first marriage produced two sons. Rarely home, he hardly knew the children, and eventually rejected both of them. Now, forced into being a "family man" by living with the Ilgenfritzes, he became "Uncle Claude" to the children. He took a special interest in Beth, the youngest.

Claude's bed consisted of two single beds pulled together to make one. He would sleep on the right bed, reserving the left one for Beth. They called it "Beth's Bed," and she could use it as a playhouse or could take naps there. He would assure her before nap time, "Do not worry; Uncle Claude your sheep dog, is here!"

As the children grew older, Claude became interested in their education, rewarding them monetarily for good grades. First, he financed their way to an exclusive private school. By the time

Beth entered kindergarten, he consented to assist Joyce and Morgan in paying the children's tuition to York (Pennsylvania) Christian School.

While at York Christian School, Beth memorized Scripture verses, learning most of them while seated next to Claude on his bed. She often recited the "ABC Gospel Train" to him: "A . . . All have sinned and fall short of the glory of God. B . . . Believe in the Lord Jesus, and you will be saved. C . . . Christ Jesus came into the world to save sinners, etc." Beth could tell Claude anything, and he claimed to visitors that he had raised her.

Claude also enjoyed Mark, the Ilgenfritzes' only son, although he was easily annoyed by his boyish behavior. Often Claude caught Mark carrying fishing poles or baseball bats to his room rather than stashing them in the closet where they belonged. Claude's room, strategically located at the bottom of the stairs that led to the children's rooms, allowed him to keep tabs on Mark. It was a rare occasion when he could sneak something by Claude.

Claude praised Shonna, the oldest child, for being the most levelheaded child of the bunch. He took pride in her academic achievements, but failed to understand her desire to become a missionary. Their relationship became particularly close, too.

Bombarded from all sides by the children's love and Christian witness, Uncle Claude could not help but be affected. When any one of the children was present, he even deleted swearing from his vocabulary—a major miracle. In spite of all his protests against their "religion," he loved the children dearly.

The one who had the biggest impact on Claude, though, was Amy, the second youngest Ilgenfritz child. She truly had a special love for "Uncle Claude." At the age of six, she had expressed a desire to sleep in Claude's house as her special birthday wish. She viewed Uncle Claude as a towering giant. Claude responded by buying a pair of pretty pink pajamas for her birthday night.

It was while Amy was still six that she accepted Jesus as her personal Savior. At the age of 10, she received the empowerment of the Holy Spirit. The Spirit gave her boldness to witness and an amazing spiritual maturity. She also evidenced a deep burden and love for Claude. At times, she would fast, earnestly praying for Claude's salvation. Because of her continual growth in the Lord, Claude felt intimidated. He called her "abnormal."

But it did not bother or deter Amy, who had a special way of sharing her love with Uncle Claude. She never went to bed without first coming into his room, kissing him good night and saying, "Good night, Uncle Claude. I love you!" This little gesture continued for years. Sometimes he would close his door and pretend to be asleep, hoping Amy would not come into his room. But she was not easily fooled. She would quietly open the door, tiptoe to his bedside, kiss his cheek and whisper, "Good night, Uncle Claude. I love you!"

A crucial confrontation occurred between Claude and Amy when she was 12. She had just spent time fasting and praying for Claude. Coming into his room, she asked permission to read him something. Thinking it homework, Claude consented. Amy started to read, "I am the way and the truth and the life. No one comes to the Father except through me." This so disturbed Claude that he grabbed the nearest thing and threw it at Amy, instantly ordering her to leave.

"Who do you think you are?" he shouted. "Only a 12-year-old, preaching at me? I never want you to come into this room and talk to me about Jesus again. I do not want to hear it!"

Although crushed by his rejection of the gospel, Amy still kept up her secret weapon—something she never missed doing—"Good night, Uncle Claude. I love you!"

CHAPTER

The Beginning

ONE DAY IN MAY 1974, Joyce was hurrying around the kitchen trying to get things ready for Amy's 13th birthday party, when the doorbell rang. "Joyce, Joyce," Claude roared from his room, "someone is ringing the doorbell off the wall."

"I hear it, Claude," Joyce replied as she ran to open the door. She swung it open and was greeted by a masculine-looking, stringy-haired young woman in baggy blue jeans.

"Good afternoon!" the young woman said. "My name is Linda. I am here representing a well-known publishing firm which manufactures and sells a wide variety of books from Bibles and Bible aids to . . ."

As the girl continued her memorized presentation, Joyce carefully scrutinized her, wondering how anyone looking like she did could possibly sell anything. As the young woman concluded her pitch, Joyce replied, "I don't believe I want any books today, but have you eaten lunch yet?"

Caught off guard, the girl answered, "Well, . . . no, I haven't, but we aren't allowed to . . ."

"Come inside," Joyce said, before she could finish. "Who will know except you, me and the Lord? Anyhow, I just returned from the grocery store and am putting away all kinds of goodies. I am sure we can find something."

Joyce fixed her a bologna sandwich and a soda, and then sat down next to her at the table. After some friendly conversation, Linda began opening up. She had just graduated from the University of Kansas and had taken this bookselling job because nothing else was available. Claude's house was her first stop.

Suddenly Joyce felt the need to witness to her. As she spoke about Jesus, Joyce sensed a tension within the girl. She finally confessed that she realiy did not know what she believed.

"Linda," Joyce said on impulse, "are you going to be here all summer?"

"Yes, that is my plan."

"Good, because I would like to be your friend!" Joyce exclaimed.

"But we aren't supposed to establish any kind of friendships while we . . ."

"Everyone needs a friend," Joyce interrupted, "and I will be yours! How about coming along with us to church Sunday?"

"Oh, I'm sorry, but I can't do that. We have our business rallies on Sunday mornings," Linda said.

"Well, just keep me in mind," Joyce replied as Linda headed for the door, "because I want to see you again."

Two weeks later, Linda returned. "Joyce," Linda confessed, "I find it very difficult talking to people, and I hate my job. Not only that, but I live with three other girls who are also selling books. We are supposed to share expenses out of our book sales commission, but I haven't made one sale! I don't even have enough money to return to Kansas."

In a comforting voice Joyce suggested, "My husband and son just left for a Boy Scout jamboree. They will be gone for three weeks. You can stay here until they return." Linda accepted, and Joyce took her to retrieve her things.

During the first week of her stay, Linda and Joyce had many discussions. On one of these occasions, Linda asked Joyce how she could be more feminine. "Well, first, you need to buy some different clothes, and then we'll have to fix up your hair and make over your face. I know, let's go on a shopping trip."

Joyce took Linda shopping, buying her a dress and shoes. Then they purchased a manicure set and other beauty aids. They went home and proceeded to work on Linda's appearance. After Joyce was finished, Linda looked at herself in the mirror. She could hardly believe the person looking back at her.

By the end of the three weeks, Linda and Joyce had become close friends. When Morgan and Mark returned from their trip, Joyce told Morgan Linda's story. Touched, Morgan agreed that she could stay. The fruit of that decision blossomed a month later when Linda accepted Jesus Christ as her Savior.

After that, things started to happen quickly for her. She secured employment at a nursing home as their activities director, joined a Bible study group and started attending church regularly. As she continued to grow in her Christian walk, she became a special member of the Ilgenfritz family, living with them for more than a year before leaving for Texas. There she signed up for intense Bible training with the Agape Force.

Her stay with the Ilgenfritzes left an impact on Joyce and Morgan. A desire to help others was born in them, and for the first time, they began to see their city through the eyes of Jesus. Linda became the first of many new Ilgenfritz family members.

Though they did not realize it at the time, the Lord was using Linda to prepare them for what lay ahead.

10

The Barriers Begin to Crumble

IT SEEMED THAT THE MORE each member of the Ilgenfritz family showed love to Claude, the more demanding and negative he became. It came to the point where he absolutely refused to hear the gospel, and he seemed to reject their love and concern as much as he could.

As an irritant to Joyce, every time the door bell or telephone rang, Claude would simultaneously ring his nurse's bell. If she did not immediately heed his call, she would be greeted by a barrage of insults and profanity. The harsher Claude became, though, the more Joyce tried to show God's love to him.

Claude would even curse her when she aided him to the bathroom. Unknown to him, though, after Joyce closed the bathroom door, she would kneel outside the door and pray for him. Every night after Claude fell asleep, Joyce would go into his room, turn off his television and kneel beside his bed and pray, "Lord Jesus, I just claim this man for You."

Then, slowly, the Lord began to break down the barriers Claude had erected in his life. This process was aided in an unexpected manner. Claude had a strong dislike for blacks, Puerto Ricans and handicapped people—anyone, really, who did not come up to his social standing or idea of perfection. But it was individuals like this who seemed to actually begin to break down Claude's defenses. While he could resist the Ilgenfritzes' love because he was used to them, he could not reject the love from someone he thought he hated.

The process had started when Linda moved in. Claude had been furious when he found out she would be living with them. He called Joyce stupid and gullible for allowing Linda to take advantage of her. And he even went as far as to say he was sure he had seen Linda's picture on television as one of the 10 most wanted women criminals in America.

During the first few weeks of Linda's stay, Claude would not even look at her. He would turn his head when she walked by his room. By the time Morgan and Mark returned from their trip, though, he was beginning to accept her and speak with her.

Linda was a clumsy person. She was always dropping things or falling down the stairs, and Claude continually made fun of her. But she was also lighthearted and never let any of Claude's remarks bother her. When she obtained employment at the convalescent home, Claude thought that was great. He dismissed his regular physical therapist and had Linda come in to exercise his legs for him. She was only too glad to do it, and soon the two came to really like one another. In Linda, Claude could not help but see Christian love in action, especially when she took time out to do special little things for him.

The second person in this process came in the spring of the next year. In March 1975, Joyce held a baby shower at the house for a black girl from New Life for Girls (a Jesus-centered ministry for young women in trouble).

Joyce and Morgan first met Brenda at a candle-light New Year's Eve church service. Joyce had recently baby-sat for Demi and Cookie Rodriquezes' children (the founders and directors of New Life for Girls) while they attended a Christmas program for the New York City Police Department. During that Christmas program, a policeman arrived handcuffed to a black girl who was seven months pregnant. Because she had experienced so many complications with her pregnancy—and her life—the Rodriquezes asked for her custody. Once they arrived back in York, though, they were not sure what do to with her. They were not set up to care for pregnant girls at their facilities. Because Joyce was a nurse and lived only six blocks away from the York Hospital, Cookie and Demi appealed to the Ilgenfritzes for assistance.

There Brenda sat in the back pew at this New Year's Eve service, shifting positions in obvious discomfort. As Joyce watched, her heart ached for Brenda. She understood her discomfort. After the service, Joyce asked Cookie for permission to take her home with them for just that evening.

After arriving home, Joyce went in to check on Claude as usual, then escorted Brenda to Amy's room, where she would sleep for the night. The next morning Brenda passed Claude's door on her way to the kitchen. Claude's bell immediately sounded.

"What just passed my door?" he inquired bois-terously.

"Why Claude, that was a pregnant girl!" Joyce replied.

"Is she black?" he barked.

"Sure!"

"I will not have a black girl living in this house," he roared.

Overhearing the conversation, Brenda later questioned Joyce about Claude's remarks. Joyce explained the situation and told her not to pay attention to him.

Even after Brenda had left, Claude continued to complain. Joyce had to once again remind him that they had invited her into their house as a guest. Morgan, as head of the house, had made the decision. Claude's complaining stopped tem-porarily.

As Brenda's delivery date approached, the Ro-driquezes again asked Joyce and Morgan if they would consider caring for her. After the phone call, Joyce looked at Morgan and said, "I think the Lord wants us to take Brenda in. She needs our help, and she needs to know the Lord. The Lord first brought Linda to our door, and now He has brought this girl. I think He's trying to tell us something. What do you think?"

Morgan had to agree, so the decision was made to invite her to live with them. When Claude found out, he went into a rage. He forbid her ad-mittance to his room and demanded that his door be closed whenever she was going to pass.

But he soon mellowed. Two weeks before her delivery, Claude began to show interest and con-cern for her. He even asked her, as she stood at his door one day, how she felt. Eventually he invited her into his room and began calling her "Honey"—his way of showing acceptance. When the new baby—named Shawn Mark after two of the Ilgenfritz children—came home, Claude permitted him to lie on his bed. "He sure is cute," he admitted to Joyce one day.

Soon it was time for Brenda to return to New Life for Girls. Before she left, Claude called her into his room to encourage her. After her departure, Joyce entered Claude's room with Shawn Mark in her arms.

"Why is Shawn still here?" he inquired.

"We are going to keep him for a year until Brenda's graduation from New Life for Girls," Joyce replied.

"You are what?" Claude exploded. "Put me in a nursing home! I never thought I wanted to go into a nursing home, but I am not going to to live under the same roof with a black baby!"

Joyce sensed that Claude's reaction was one of jealousy instead of dislike for the child. He feared that the baby would take up some of the time Joyce spent waiting on him.

When Morgan arrived home that evening and learned of Claude's response, he became upset himself. In a rare outburst, he angrily informed Claude, "We will place a 'For Sale' sign in the yard tomorrow, sell the house and settle our differences. You can move into a nursing home. If we have to move into a shack, we will. Shawn *is* staying with us!"

Claude sensed Morgan's seriousness, and immediately relented, apologizing for his outburst. As Joyce had suspected, his attitude about the

baby changed. He even developed a special relationship with the little boy. When Joyce put
Shawn's playpen by the window, Claude meas-
ured his growth by comparing his height to the
window sill.

Shortly after Shawn's departure, Joyce became
acquainted with the third person in Claude's soft-
ening process. She was another young woman
from New Life for Girls, a Puerto Rican named
Lucy. Lucy had just had her leg amputated. The
Rodriquezes had asked Joyce to visit Lucy in the
hospital, and she did. During the visit, Joyce saw
that there was another problem with Lucy, too.
She was facially deformed. When she was young,
someone had thrown lye on her.

Joyce could sense that the Rodriquezes did not
know what to do with Lucy upon her release from
the hospital. Because the New Life for Girls facilities were in the country, Lucy would be quite a
distance from medical help. She also sensed that
they were hoping she and Morgan would consider
taking her in.

After two weeks of prayer, Joyce approached
Morgan about the situation. "I have to ask you
something," she said.

"I know what you are going to ask," he said,
catching Joyce by surprise. "Just today I told the
guys at work that I bet that you will want to bring
Lucy home."

Under her breath Joyce murmured, "Thank
You, Jesus!" Now only one major barrier re-
mained—Claude. She knew he disliked Puerto
Ricans.

During a casual conversation with him one
morning, Joyce, sensing his good mood, began to

talk about Lucy. "Claude, I have been to the hospital to visit a girl who just had her leg amputated. She is Spanish."

"Oh, Spanish!" he exclaimed. "Spanish women are beautiful!"

Joyce agreed, as he rambled on about bull-fights and the like. Then she informed him, "Morgan and I have decided to bring her here to live while she recuperates. What do you think?"

"What do I think?" he chuckled. "I have been around you long enough to know that you are going to do it regardless of what I think."

"Does that mean I have your approval?" Joyce quickly pressed.

"I guess so."

When Lucy came to the Ilgenfritz home, Joyce introduced her to Claude. Immediately after they left his room, he rang for Joyce.

"What do you mean by bringing that girl home? Spanish! Are you kidding? She is a Puerto Rican!"

"Spanish and Puerto Rican are the same," Joyce suggested.

"What happened to her face?" he continued. "She has only one eye!"

Again Joyce explained, "She had lye thrown in her face when she was 14 years old."

"You mean to tell me that you are going to have that deformed girl live in this house?" he scoffed.

Again, though, love broke through. Every night, Morgan and Mark would carry Lucy upstairs to sleep in Amy's room. Each morning she would hobble down the steps, lean against Claude's door and say, in the sweetest voice, "Good morning Uncle Claude. How are you?"

At first he would only stare out the window saying, "OK," not wanting to have to look at her, but finally he melted. The morning he said, "Honey, how are you feeling?" Joyce ran to her bedroom in jubilation, praising Jesus. The relationship warmed, and Lucy became Claude's special friend.

The Lord works in truly marvelous ways. As He brought into the Ilgenfritz home a succession of hurting, needy young people, He used them to soften Claude's recalcitrant heart. But beyond that, He was impressing on Joyce and Morgan a sense of the continuing ministry He wanted them to have. Claude's house with its ample space would become a lighthouse where these individuals could find Jesus, the Light of the world. And the two light keepers, obedient to the heavenly vision, responded wholeheartedly.

CHAPTER
11

A Special Gift

IN OCTOBER 1975, Joyce and Morgan traveled to Shonna's college for Parent's Day—the first time they had been away together since moving into Claude's house. One of Joyce's sisters and her husband stayed with Claude, and Lucy went to New Life for Girls for the weekend.

On their return home, Joyce and Morgan were alarmed to find a sudden relapse in Claude's health. Joyce began to despair. She realized that Claude might not have long to live, yet he still had not accepted Jesus as his Savior. She began to wonder what else she could do.

Claude had heard the gospel many times. Joyce had held weekly Bible studies in her home. Although Claude did not participate, he lay in his room listening intently. After all the women had gone, Claude would critique Joyce's presentations. The gospel had to be penetrating!

On another occasion, Joyce had brought a blind couple into Claude's room. When they sang, "How Great Thou Art," tears filled Claude's eyes. After they left, though, Claude told Joyce, "Don't you ever bring those handicapped people into my room again!"

Whenever he knew that preachers were coming to visit the Ilgenfritzes, he ordered Joyce and

Morgan, "Lock my door and pull the blinds. I don't want to see anybody."

Now, with time running out for Claude, Joyce could not see God at work.

A day or so later, Claude summoned Joyce to his room. He had something concealed in his hand. When Joyce sat on the end of the bed, he paid her a rare compliment. "You have been pretty good to me lately. I heard that you are taking Lucy shopping this afternoon. Here, I want you to take this."

He dropped a $10 bill into Joyce's hand. "I want you to buy yourself a present. Every time you go shopping you buy something for the kids or someone else. I want you to spend this on yourself."

Thanking Claude, Joyce left to prepare for the shopping trip. She loaded Lucy and her wheelchair into the car and headed to the local department store. As she pushed Lucy through the store, Claude's words, "You have been pretty good to me, go buy yourself a present" kept going through her mind.

Joyce looked at Lucy and said, "You know, this is going to be the most important present I will ever buy."

"You mean a present for yourself?" she inquired. "How can that be?"

"The moment I get home from shopping, Claude will ask me what I bought. It's got to count because Uncle Claude is going to die soon, and this might be the last present he ever gives me."

While searching for something to buy, Joyce noticed several large pictures priced at $9.99. All were pictures of Jesus. One was entitled, *Jesus Kneeling at the Garden of Gethsemane*. Another was *Jesus Holding the Little Lost Sheep* and a third, *Jesus and the Children*. Then, Joyce spotted a fourth one. "Lucy, that's it! I want to buy that picture!" Joyce exclaimed, pushing Lucy toward a picture named *Jesus, Knocking at the Door*. Like the others, it too cost $9.99—right within her budget! Joyce knew Claude just had to see this picture.

Arriving home, Joyce could hardly control herself. She hung the picture in the hallway just outside Claude's bedroom door. As soon as he asked about her purchase, she would quickly show it to him.

"Hello!" Joyce chirped, peeking her head into his room.

"I want my medicine," Claude demanded.

Disappointed, Joyce brought him his medicine. Maybe he would ask her about the purchase later. Finally, almost a week later, Claude asked Joyce what she had bought with the $10.

Joyce responded excitedly, "I bought something really nice. Let me show you."

Joyce retrieved the painting from the hall and held it up for Claude to see. "What do you think of it?"

Claude blurted out a profanity, then proceeded to tell Joyce, "You remind me of one of those dumb Polacks who live in Western Pennsylvania. They all have a picture of Christ hanging in their living rooms."

"Oh, but I think it's really a good picture," Joyce hastily observed, ignoring his comment.

"Have you ever heard the story behind this picture?"

Before he could answer, Joyce started the story. "Jesus is standing at this door knocking. Do you notice that there is no doorknob? Jesus is such a gentleman that He would never force Himself onto anyone. That door represents our lives. In order for Jesus to come into our hearts, we must open the door from the inside."

Noticing tears in Claude's eyes, Joyce talked even faster. "You know, Claude, this represents Jesus knocking at *your* heart, waiting for *you* to open the door."

Suddenly a drastic change came over Claude. Piece by piece, he began throwing everything on his end table at Joyce, including the entire contents of the coffee pot. "Get out of here!" he screamed at the top of his lungs, all red-faced and coughing and choking. "Do not ever mention the name of Jesus to me again!"

Backing into the hallway with the picture in her hand, Joyce cleared her throat, "Claude, I promise never to talk to you about Jesus again, but I want you to know that I will never stop talking to Jesus about you."

Soon after that, Claude's condition worsened, and he needed round-the-clock care. Joyce told Lucy she would have to return to New Life for Girls, because she just would not have the time to care for her. Then Claude slipped into a coma. Joyce called the doctor, who, after examining him, predicted he would die before morning.

The horrible sound of Claude's troubled breathing was audible throughout the house. Upset, Joyce remembered the scriptural promise God had earlier given her concerning Claude. In spite of feeling drained physically, mentally and spiritually, she began to pray once again for him, holding onto that promise of God to answer the one who calls on Him (Jeremiah 33:3).

That afternoon, Joyce telephoned a friend of the family, Pastor John Oldfield of Yorktowne Chapel, who prayed with her over the phone. During his prayer, he asked that Satan would be bound. Following his prayer he advised her, "Joyce, you have to take spiritual authority over Satan. I sincerely believe that evil powers are fighting for Claude's soul."

That evening Claude's condition deteriorated, and the children were upset as they went to bed, aware that Claude could die at any moment. As Morgan and Joyce sat in the living room, they heard Amy sobbing in her room. Morgan suggested, "Honey, why don't you go up to Amy? She needs you."

When Joyce entered Amy's room, she found her on her knees praying. "Oh, dear Jesus, don't let Uncle Claude die. He does not know You."

With tears in her eyes, Joyce knelt beside Amy, joining her in prayer. Suddenly, an unexplainable peace came over them both. Never had they experienced anything like it before.

"I believe Uncle Claude will be all right now," Joyce said, putting her arm around Amy.

"I know, Mother," Amy agreed. She stopped crying, crawled into bed and went to sleep.

Back downstairs, Joyce stopped to check on Claude. She saw him in the dim light, his body breathing with irregular, heavy, rattling breaths.

Looking at him that night was like staring into the face of death.

Joyce walked quietly to the side of the bed. Remembering what Pastor Oldfield had earlier instructed her about taking spiritual authority over Satan, she looked at Claude and commanded, "Devil, you are not getting Claude. He belongs to God."

Immediately one of the most horrible expressions she had ever seen appeared on his face. His jaw jutted out, and his face contorted. Then an evil growl, like that of a mad dog, came out of his mouth. Joyce backed against the wall, frozen in fear.

Morgan rushed into the room, "Was that the dog growling?" he asked.

"No," Joyce gasped, still standing against the wall, "that came from Claude."

Turning toward Claude, Joyce again commanded, "In the name of Jesus, leave this man. Get out of here." Again Claude's face contorted, and another growl escaped his lips. This sequence continued a total of nine times. The last time Claude let out a violent choking grunt, then his body relaxed, and he fell into his normal state of sleep.

Morgan and Joyce stood by his bed in awe. God had answered prayer. Finally, Morgan said, "Why don't we go to bed. Everything will be all right now."

The next morning, the children asked about Uncle Claude while they got ready for school. Joyce smiled as she reported that his breathing had returned to normal. As the children boarded the school bus, Claude's bell rang, and Joyce hurried to his room.

"I am awfully sick," Claude whispered as Joyce leaned over his bed to hear him.

"I know," Joyce whispered back. "You almost died last night."

"Did I?" he said, looking surprised.

As Joyce washed his faced with a warm cloth, she looked compassionately at him and said, "Claude, if you had died last night, it would have been the last time we would have seen you. We love you, but God loves you even more. I know I promised you I would never again talk to you about Jesus, but I must!"

Opening his eyes, he uttered the most beautiful words Joyce had ever heard, "I am ready." Joining Joyce in the sinner's prayer, Claude confessed his sins, asked Jesus' forgiveness and invited Him to come into his heart.

As she left Claude's room with tear-filled eyes, Morgan embraced her. Thinking the worse, he inquired, "Did Claude die?"

Through tears of joy, Joyce sobbed, "No, Morgan, Claude did not die. He just received life! He just received Jesus into his heart!" Both rejoiced in the "great and mighty things (KJV)" that God had done. God had fulfilled His promise in His own way and time.

Joyce then decided to call her own pastor, David Muir, with the good news. He too had long been praying for Claude's salvation. Before she got to the telephone, it rang. To Joyce's astonishment, she heard, "Hello, this is Pastor Muir."

"Oh, Pastor Muir. I was about to call you. I have

great news. Claude just accepted Jesus as his Lord and Savior!"

"Praise the Lord," he said. "I will be right there." Within minutes he arrived. Only once before had Pastor Muir been permitted in Claude's presence. This time, however, Claude greeted him with a weak, but friendly, "Hi, Preach!"

"I just heard the good news," Pastor Muir said as he walked to Claude's bed. "As I was driving here, I thought of Psalm 23. 'The Lord is my shepherd . . .'"

"'I shall not want. He maketh me to lie down in green pastures: he leadeth me beside the still waters. He restoreth my soul: . . .'" Claude continued as he recited the rest of the 23rd Psalm perfectly.

Pastor Muir, Claude, Morgan and Joyce joined hands while Pastor Muir prayed. As the pastor turned to leave, Claude actually thanked him for coming.

Claude lived for four more days, wanting only the Bible read to him. Joyce's voice soon became hoarse, but her mother and sisters came to her aid and read all four Gospels to Claude. His whole countenance had changed. Just prior to this, Claude had taken Demerol every two or three hours around the clock on doctor's orders, but the last four days he would knock the syringe out of Joyce's hands when she offered him shots.

"I am ready to die," he said with an expression of newfound peace on his face.

His life had a fairy-tale ending. Shonna, who had come home from college for a week to help her mother care for Claude, said goodbye to him about four o'clock that afternoon before leaving to return to college. He kissed her goodbye and, still proud of her as ever, wished her well.

That night, Mark bid what was to be his final good night to Claude as he headed up the stairs to his room.

When Beth came to say, "Good night, Uncle Claude," he took her by the hand, and gave her his farewell blessing, "Sweetheart, I love you."

Amy then came in and stood at the foot of his bed, "Good night, Uncle Claude. I love you! I won't kiss you tonight because I have a cold. I will throw you a kiss instead!"

After she saw the children to bed, Joyce came back down to Claude's room. As she bent over him to adjust his pillows, she brushed against his face. "Your nose is cold," she said.

"Don't you know healthy dogs have cold noses?" he replied, still able to show a sense of humor.

Upstairs Beth began reading a nursery rhyme book. Claude had worked so hard to help her with reading. Morgan brewed a cup of tea in the kitchen, while Joyce sat on Claude's bed listening to his steady breathing. The monotony of his breathing made her drowsy, and she dozed off.

As she slept, Joyce dreamed that she saw Claude standing in his room wearing a big white nightshirt with tails. On the door she noticed a plaque inscribed with these words, "This room is dedicated to the glory of God in memory of Claude J. Banks."

Joyce awoke with a start and raced down the stairs to Morgan, describing her dream to him. Morgan went to check on Claude and soon came back. "It is all over, honey," he said. "Claude is dead."

Returning to Claude's room, Joyce and Morgan stood by his bedside, weeping tears of quiet victory. Instead of the awful, contorted face of a few days earlier, Claude now wore a peaceful smile.

Claude's sister and brother came to stay with the Ilgenfritz family during his funeral. Both of his sons also attended, keeping a close eye on everything. Later that night, the phone rang. As Joyce picked up the phone, she received a momentary shock. A voice that sounded like Claude's said, "If you people are for real, then God bless you." It was his oldest son affirming Joyce and Morgan's relationship with his father.

A few days later, they received a sympathy card in the mail. It was from one of Claude's oldest friends. As Joyce opened it up and read the words, tears came to her eyes. At the funeral, he had heard Pastor Muir's sermon on Claude's 11th-hour conversion. The Holy Spirit spoke to him, and he accepted Christ as his Savior. In the card, he thanked Joyce and Morgan for their impact on Claude's life—and ultimately on his!

Again, Joyce praised the Lord for His faithfulness in saving Claude and for the verse in Jeremiah, "Call unto me, and I will answer thee, and shew thee great and mighty things, which thou knowest not" (KJV).

CHAPTER

12

An "Angelic" Visitation

RIGHT AFTER CLAUDE'S DEATH, Joyce and Morgan attended a missionary convention at their church. They both felt sure that God was calling them to a special ministry and somehow felt that it involved their home, but they needed assurance from God. In his message, the missionary speaker talked about the need for full-time workers. At the close of the service, he gave an invitation, and the two of them at once rose to their feet. That night they said, "Yes, Lord, we are willing. We are willing to do anything that You might have for us. We will go wherever You want us to go."

Excited about their new commitment, Joyce and Morgan were anxious to see what the Lord had in store for them. Perhaps He was calling them to overseas service.

But the Lord did not take them across the seas. Instead, He brought the mission field to them. Over the years, the Ilgenfritz home welcomed a stream of new faces. God gave Joyce and Morgan a new desire to help those in need. Soon they dedicated their house to His use, naming it "The Lighthouse." Their desire was that they might be a lighthouse showing forth God's light to their neighborhood and community. Claude's old bedroom—with the dedication plaque Joyce envisioned in her dream installed on the door—became a special guest room for overnight or short-term visitors, and the actual house received numerous structural changes and remodeling to accommodate the needs of the various visitors.

In the following two years, Joyce and Morgan became "grandparents" to six infants. Because of their earlier experience with Brenda, Joyce agreed to work with New Life for Girls to care for pregnant girls during their last trimester of pregnancy. She would coach them through labor and delivery, and for six weeks after delivery, she would help each new mother learn to care for her new baby before returning to New Life for Girls.

The first of these mothers-to-be was a girl named Andrea. Andrea had been a gang member in New York City and had served time in prison. Her husband had also been a gang member, and he, too, had been in jail. Both had made commitments to Christ through outreach ministries in the prisons.

From the first day at The Lighthouse, all Andrea could talk about was her husband, Angel. Morgan eventually gave her permission to talk to him on the telephone. Because Andrea was scheduled for a Caesarean delivery, the Ilgenfritzes made plans for Angel to be with his wife on the day of the delivery.

On one of those rainy, cold, January mornings, when one would rather stay indoors than venture outside, Joyce and Andrea drove to the bus terminal to meet Angel. Arriving at the terminal, Joyce began searching for this "angelic" fellow. Andrea, heavy with child, slowly crawled out of the car, calling, "Angel, Angel!" She caught the attention of a young man who ran to embrace her.

As Joyce turned to meet him, she experienced a real shock! Angel wore a leather jacket and blue jeans, had shoulder-length hair covered by a stocking cap, sported a mustache and beard and boasted of being half Chinese and half Puerto Rican. He even wore an earring. His appearance was just short of frightening!

As they all climbed into the car, Joyce asked him, "Did you have any lunch yet?"

"No, not yet," he replied.

"Good, let's stop at McDonalds," Joyce suggested.

As Joyce drove toward the restaurant, only the swish-swish sound of the windshield wipers could be heard as the rain increased in intensity. Looking in her rearview mirror, Joyce glanced at the two. Their constant embracing did not bother her, but his wearing an earring did. Somewhere in her mind, she remembered hearing that members of gangs wore earrings.

"I see you wear an earring," she finally said. "Does it have any special meaning?"

"No," he quickly replied.

"I always heard that if you wore an earring, you were a member of a gang."

"Sometimes that is true," he acknowledged.

"Oh, . . . are you a member of a gang?" Joyce asked.

"Nope!" he said.

The conversation came to an end as they pulled into McDonalds. They went inside, ordered their food and sat down at a table. Angel politely asked Joyce, "Would you like to pray?" Somewhat taken aback, Joyce complied.

After Angel finished eating, he excused himself and went to the restroom. His wife bent over the table and spoke to Joyce. "I can tell that you are troubled by his earring," she said.

"Yes," Joyce confessed, "around here you don't see that kind of thing."

Andrea quickly explained, "Angel made a promise to the Lord that he would wear that earring until we had another daughter. You see, our prison sentences came about because while we were high on drugs we scalded our two-year-old daughter to death during a bath."

Joyce did not know what to say. As they drove to the hospital, Joyce wondered where Angel would spend the night. She really did not want him staying in her home. Then, she overheard him tell his wife that he planned to stay at the YMCA. As Joyce left the couple at the hospital, Angel asked if he could possibly have supper with them before he went to the YMCA that night.

"Sure," Joyce said, agreeing to pick him up.

When Joyce arrived home, she asked Morgan, "What do you think about Angel's staying at the YMCA? It is quite a distance from the hospital, and he has no transportation."

"I would feel better if he stayed here," Morgan answered. A short time later, the telephone rang. It was Angel. He was ready to be picked up.

When Joyce returned with Angel, it was time for dinner. Everyone bowed his head as Morgan led in prayer. As he prayed, Angel began to weep. At the conclusion of the prayer, Angel rose from his seat and walked around the table to Morgan. He threw his arms around him and wept openly. They were now assured that Jesus had indeed directed this young man to their home.

The next morning, while preparing for the trip to the hospital, Joyce turned on the "700 Club." As Angel entered the room, Pat Robertson was talking about prayer. "We should pray for young married couples. There is one married couple in particular who has had a lot of trouble in their past and just needs a healing. There is somebody watching today who needs that," Robertson said. Joyce and Angel held hands in agreement with Pat Robertson's prayer, and God began to work on this young man's heart.

They arrived at the hospital just in time for Angel to see his wife being transported into the operating room. The doctor advised them to wait by the operating room doors. "In about a half an hour, you should see your baby," he told Angel.

The doors finally swung open, and the doctor announced, "It's a girl!"

Angel reached to his ear, removed his earring and threw it in a nearby trash basket. He had fulfilled his promise!

On Sunday, Morgan invited Angel to go to church with them. Angel accepted, but he told Joyce and Morgan that he had never been inside a church. When Angel appeared with his black T-shirt and blue jeans, Joyce became concerned. She was afraid that he would feel awkward and self-conscious in church.

"Angel, would you be offended if Morgan gave you one of his shirts and a tie to wear to church?"

"No, I wouldn't," Angel responded.

Morgan brought Angel one of his shirts, a pair of trousers and a tie. Shortly Angel returned for assistance. "Morgan, I don't know how to tie a tie," he said. "I haven't worn one since I was six years old, and then I didn't tie it myself. Can you help me?"

"Come over here, son," Morgan replied. "I will tie your tie!" When Morgan called him son, Angel's eyes welled with tears.

The Sunday school lesson that morning spoke to Angel. The teacher dramatically portrayed the crucifixion of Jesus and how the nails pierced His hands. Afterward, Angel looked at Joyce and said, "My heart hurts!"

Is Angel going to have a heart attack? she asked herself. For a minute, Joyce did not understand what he meant.

"My heart hurts when I think of those nails that went into Jesus' hands," he went on to say. "I never heard anyone explain it like that!"

After lunch everyone visited Angel's wife and new daughter. Andrea could not believe that Angel had worn a shirt and tie to church. Later that evening Angel asked Joyce, "Do you think Morgan could lend me a razor? Looking around in church today, I didn't see anyone who looked like me. Being a new father, I want to look like the other men."

Morgan gave Angel a razor, and he disappeared into the bathroom. When he finally emerged, he was clean shaven, and his hair was trimmed.

Soon mother and daughter came home from the hospital, and the new parents and their daughter lived at The Lighthouse for three months before leaving. It was a special time for both families. Angel and Andrea grew in their faith, and Joyce and Morgan became more assured of God's plan for their home and lives.

CHAPTER

CHAPTER

13

Five Newborns at Once!

AFTER ANGEL AND HIS family left The Light-house, things settled down for a month or two. Summer came, though, and with it, *four* mothers-to-be!

The first to arrive was a cute Puerto Rican girl named Debbie, who came from a family of 15 children. Her mother was a practicing witch who used to beat Debbie with an extension cord, leaving her permanently scarred.

At first, Debbie was shy and said little. It was several weeks before she gained confidence in the Ilgenfritzes, but that confidence soon developed into a real love and trust.

Two weeks before the birth of Debbie's baby, she and Joyce purchased a number of diapers. To-gether with what baby clothes had already been collected, they washed the new diapers. In fact, Debbie washed the clothes and diapers three or four times before the little one arrived—just for practice! Often Joyce would find her in the laun-dry room refolding her stack of diapers.

About this time, Pam, the second expectant mother, arrived. Pam came from a well-to-do Ital-ian family. She had run away from home at the age of 16 and had become involved with the Hell's Angels motorcycle gang. She eventually married one of the gang members, who was now in prison for drug offenses. Pam had been using drugs since she was 13.

Joyce and Morgan decided to let the two girls room together. How different they were: one came from a poor, abusive home, the other from an affluent family. Now they found themselves in the same situation—pregnant—and it proved to be a bonding point between them.

Shortly after moving into The Lighthouse, Pam learned that she was going to have twins! Somehow, though, the news failed to delight her.

The third expectant mother was a black girl named Anna. Anna had been born and raised in Alabama, but she now lived in New York City. Her Southern ways and accent, however, remained with her.

Two girls were fine, but now three? Joyce and Morgan were not sure they could manage three, but they decided to give it a try. Just as they were making arrangements, Debbie went into labor and gave birth. For the moment, the problems of making space for the third mother-to-be were forgotten. The entire household rejoiced over the new birth. The two other girls doted on the infant and talked about what their babies would be like.

One day soon after this, Joyce received a telephone call. Could she possibly make room for a *fourth* girl? A fourth pregnant girl! Joyce could not believe she heard herself telling the caller it would be OK. The next day the expectant mother, another girl from the South, arrived. Her name was Brenda, but she acquired the nickname

"Cornbread" during her stay at The Lighthouse because of all the cornbread she made and ate while living there. Her problems started when a carnival came to her hometown. One of the carnival employees persuaded her to have sex with him, promising her that he would take her with him when the carnival pulled out. Of course, he left, and she soon discovered that she was pregnant. Afraid to tell her parents, she did not know what to do. Then someone told her about New Life for Girls, and here she was.

The arrival of the fourth girl necessitated immediate changes. The excitement over the first baby had subsided by now, and the household was back to the task of day-to-day living. Problems naturally arose—three pregnant women, one new mother and her baby and the Ilgenfritz family were bound to meet each other once in a while in the house!

One panacea for potential confrontations between the girls was a time of daily devotions, led by Joyce. Tensions between the girls seemed to disintegrate as they read God's Word and prayed together.

One day, though, Joyce sensed something was wrong. There seemed to be an electric current of tension in the air. Joyce had noticed in particular that Anna and Brenda—who were rooming together—were acting strangely. Dissension could be seen in their attitudes and looks toward one another.

The situation erupted one evening as the two of them were watching a television program about the South and the Ku Klux Klan. Brenda, who was white, claimed that the Ku Klux Klan was a

Christian organization which aided people in need. She went on to proclaim proudly that her father was the head of the local group back in her home county. Anna, who was black, reacted in rage.

The verbal battle climaxed when Joyce, worrying that it might bring on labor, interrupted, shouting, "All right girls, this has got to stop! No one is going to bed until this is settled. I do not care if it takes until four in the morning!"

Even after talking through the problem and prayer, bad feelings still existed. Joyce reminded them, "The Bible says, 'Do not let the sun go down while you are still angry' (Ephesians 4:26). This is God's house. We cannot have a disagreement like this. We are allowing the devil to do his thing, and we are feeling the effects of it. Since it is getting late, and we are tired, why don't you two just hug each other in forgiveness?"

"You think I am going to hug her?" the white girl scoffed.

"Yes, I do," Joyce firmly replied.

Finally, the two did exchange a hug, but Joyce could see Brenda's insincerity. "Hug her like you mean it," Joyce said. "Tell her you love her!"

Suddenly convicted, she did, and the love of Jesus broke through as repentance filled both girls. After that, they became good friends, constantly caring for each other. Only Christ's love could have brought those two girls—from backgrounds of hatred—together and molded them into sisters of love.

One by one, Pam, Anna and Brenda had their babies—Pam giving birth to healthy twins. Two weeks before each girl's delivery, Joyce had each

one memorize Philippians 4:13, "I can do everything through him who gives me strength." During labor, Joyce had each girl recite the verse,
asking, "It says I can do what?"

"Everything," the girl would answer.

"That's right, not *some* things, but *every-*
thing!" Joyce would continue by asking, "What
are you doing right now?"

"I'm having a baby."

"That's right! And you can have that baby
through Christ Jesus' strength. You won't have to
put up a big fuss."

When experiencing strong contractions, the
girl would whimper, "I can do everything through
him who gives me strength."

Joyce would coach them all through labor, encouraging them to recite the verse. It was such a
testimony in the labor room that the doctors and
nurses commented on how The Lighthouse girls
were their best patients.

Now The Lighthouse had five babies, four
mothers and some more adjusting to do. Joyce
agreed to cook the meals, clean the house and
give them help as needed, but the mothers had to
care for their own babies. They could sleep during the day when their babies slept, but they had
to get up with them at night. No way was Joyce
going to play mother for five babies at three
o'clock in the morning!

The babies were exceptionally good, though—
a blessing, considering the crowded conditions.
Never once did all five cry at the same time. Problems developed, however, because the mothers
were constantly "borrowing" each other's bottles
and formula. To solve this, Joyce designated a

location for each baby's supplies, and only that baby's mother could take supplies from that location.

Evenings became warm and loving times. Each baby had his or her own cradle in the living room, and after supper, all four mothers would gather there to prepare their babies for bed. They would laugh and play with the infants and talk about future plans.

Another important part of each day came at five o'clock in the afternoon. That was when Morgan came home from work. All four girls made a special effort to be in the kitchen just when he came through the door, to hear him say, "Hello!" Then they would make it a point to stay and watch as he gave Joyce a kiss. Their expressions of love and unity in Christ proved to be a modeling for the girls of what a Christ-centered marriage could be like.

Handling the babies became a matter of diplomacy. If Morgan talked to one baby, he had to talk to the others. If he held one, he eventually had to hold them all—or confront a jealous mother!

Too soon the time came for each girl to leave. As each one left, the others shed tears as they realized that they would probably not see each other again. It was amazing to see how close they had become and how each had matured into a beautiful Christian young woman. It was also amazing to see how God had supplied needs. When each girl came to The Lighthouse, she brought her entire earthly possessions in a bag. She had nothing for her baby. But when each girl got ready to leave, a station wagon was required to take away the baby's layette.

Joyce and the girls had prayed that God would supply their needs, and He did. Donations from friends, neighbors, church members and others kept the baby chest supplied at The Lighthouse. What a testimony of God's faithfulness this was to the girls—and to Joyce and Morgan!

CHAPTER
14

A Heart's Desire

BECAUSE OF THE NATURE of the Ilgenfritzes' ministry, married couples staying at The Lighthouse were a rarity. The extra rooms were usually full of unwed mothers or wayward youths or those just needing a place to stay for a while.

Joyce and Morgan had become friends with a couple, Tony and Debbie, who lived in one of the apartments across the street. One day the couple came over to visit. They had been married for over a year and were now seeking the Lord's guidance for the next step in their lives. They had contracted to rent a large farmhouse south of York. Their present landlord had found someone else to rent the apartment and wanted them to vacate it within a short time. They could not move into the farmhouse for several weeks and so had no place to live. Could they possibly move into The Lighthouse for that period of time?

"Right now we are rather full," Joyce explained (the last of four mothers was nearing her time to leave), "but Brenda should be leaving about the time you need to vacate your apartment. I think we could let you come. What do you think, Morgan?"

"Well," Morgan teased with a serious look on his face, "I don't know." Then, smiling, he said, "I only ask one thing of you. You have to become part of the family. If you raided the refrigerator at your home, feel free to raid it here. We are all family, so you need to make yourselves right at home."

So at the appointed time, Tony and Debbie moved into Claude's old bedroom. That first night, Joyce decided to have some fun. She hid a pair of baby booties under their pillows.

The next morning at the breakfast table, Joyce hid her smirking smile behind her coffee cup. Finally, they held up the booties and asked Joyce if she knew anything about them. Joyce's sheepish looks gave her away as they all laughed.

Debbie was not working at the time, and she assisted Joyce in her daily chores—a seemingly endless routine necessary to keep The Lighthouse functioning. As they were preparing the evening meal one afternoon, the baby booties became a topic of conversation. "Do you think you will ever have children?" Joyce asked.

"I don't know," Debbie responded. "Tony wants children, but I don't think I do."

"Really," Joyce said, surprised. "Why?"

"My father was in the Navy," Debbie confessed, "and I remember all those ladies who were pregnant. They didn't keep themselves neat, and they were always alone because their husbands were at sea."

"But that's not the case with you and Tony," Joyce replied.

"I know, but I'm just not ready for children," Debbie honestly replied.

Several weeks later, Joyce invited Debbie to a Christian women's dinner. Needing a change of outlook, Debbie gladly accepted. The message that night happened to be about the woman's role as wife, mother and homemaker.

After the meeting, Joyce and Debbie talked about what the speaker said. Joyce could tell that the message had had an effect on Debbie. They prayed together, then Debbie went to the bedroom and returned to the kitchen with a plastic packet in her hand. With Joyce as her witness, she threw away her birth control pills, proclaiming that she was going to put her trust in the Lord concerning the matter of having children. That night she would share her new trust with her husband and ask Jesus to put the desire for children into her heart, cleansing her of the preconceived ideas she held.

Soon the couple left to occupy their new home. Nearly two years later, the good news reached The Lighthouse that Debbie was pregnant.

Debbie came to York Hospital for the baby's birth. Last minute complications necessitated a Caesarean delivery, and her stay in the hospital was extended an additional two days giving Joyce opportunity to visit mother and baby—a boy. As the week progressed, the baby became jaundiced and had to remain hospitalized an additional day. The concern for her baby was taking its toll on Debbie, and Joyce offered her and Tony use of the guest room.

So The Lighthouse again became this couple's temporary home. In fact, the new baby spent his first out-of-the-hospital nights there before Tony and Debbie returned to their home in the country. The arrival of this new human life brought celebration to The Lighthouse. The baby was placed in the wooden cradle that had already held so many other babies, and the cradle was placed in the very room where those baby booties were first planted!

15

A Special Wedding

ALTHOUGH MANY OF The Lighthouse's guests were young people from problem backgrounds, not all fell into this category. One special friend of the Ilgenfritzes was a girl named Nancy. Joyce knew her parents when she was a little girl. As a teenager, she became a regular visitor at The Lighthouse and even asked Joyce if she could come on Sunday afternoons and spend time in prayer. The presence of God could be felt there, she told Joyce when making this request.

Nancy actually started coming before Claude's death and became a prayer warrior for his salvation. Her residence at The Lighthouse began early in 1978 while she attended school at York College. One Sunday, shortly after she moved in, she announced her engagement to the Ilgenfritzes. She and her fiance, Roger, were planning a June wedding.

Just seeing Nancy's wedding gown hanging in the room excited Joyce. The night before her wedding, Nancy asked that Joyce and Morgan pray with her—that the wedding would go smoothly and that her marriage would be successful.

Before they all went to bed that evening, Joyce said to her, "I want to give you something special from my home as a wedding gift. You can have anything in the house you wish. Just ask for it, and it's yours!"

"I will have to think about that," she responded. "I will let you know in the morning."

The next morning, Joyce, curious to know what she had decided, asked, "Have you made up your mind?"

"I prayed about it last night," she said smilingly, "and decided that there is something I would like. Could I have those praying hands on your end table? I want them so that I will always be reminded of our praying together the night before my wedding."

The wedding was scheduled for the afternoon. After the wedding, Nancy wanted to have photographs taken by the fountain in the yard beside the Ilgenfritz house. But as Joyce looked outside that morning, she doubted that this would be possible. It was raining, and the forecast for the day was more rain.

This did not seem to bother the young bride-to-be, though. "Well praise the Lord!" she said when Joyce told her of the weather forecast. "It will stop raining in time for my pictures. The Lord has already told me that I would be able to have the pictures taken in your yard."

It rained during the entire wedding service. Toward the end, however, the rain tapered off. Looking outside after the service, Nancy told the wedding party, "Let's go to Joyce's for our pictures." So everything was loaded up, and the group drove to The Lighthouse.

Upon their arrival, Nancy hopped out of the car and headed toward the fountain in the side yard.

As she did, the clouds parted overhead, and the sun came out, shining right down on the fountain and the happy couple. The background for the shot was even better than what a clear day could have offered! The raindrops, still clinging to the grass and trees, added an air of freshness and newness to the scene.

After the last photograph was shot, Nancy looked heavenward in praise and said, "Thank You, Father! I knew that I could have my pictures taken here."

As the wedding party loaded back up and headed for the reception, the sky clouded over again and it began to drizzle.

CHAPTER
16

Thank You for Caring

ONE MORNING AS MORGAN stood drying his hands by the kitchen sink, the phone rang. "Hello, Ilgenfritzes," he answered.

"Morgan, this is Wendy (not her real name)!" said the voice at the other end. "You probably don't remember me, but I'm the girl your wife picked up alongside the road near York College."

"Yes, I remember you," Morgan said.

"Is Joyce home?" Wendy asked.

"No, I'm sorry, but she's not," Morgan answered.

"Well, I just had to call and thank you again for what you did for me. Three weeks after I arrived at my sister's house, my sister and her husband were killed in a head-on car collision. Since then, for some reason, I have been thinking of you and Joyce." She paused, her voice choked with emotion. "If not for my personal relationship with Jesus, I could not have faced this tragedy. I am so grateful for the three weeks that I spent with my sister after leaving The Lighthouse."

It had been just two months since that crisp autumn day in October when Wendy arrived at The Lighthouse. Joyce had been on her way to

83

the York Hospital to visit her mother in the coronary care unit.

The road to the hospital passed by York College. As she approached the area, she could see the campus alive with activity. Students scurried here and there, some jogging, some on their way to class, others just lounging about. One girl in particular, though, caught Joyce's eye. She seemed somehow out of place. In spite of the morning chill, she wore only a halter top and a pair of short shorts. She was barefoot. Huddled by the side of the road, she watched with great uncertainity as cars sped by her.

On the way back home, Joyce noticed the girl still standing in the same spot, watching each vehicle as attentively as before. Joyce resisted the urge to stop and offer assistance. She knew that she would pass by the campus again that afternoon on her second daily visit to her mother. Maybe then, if the girl was still there, she would stop.

After lunch, Joyce returned to the hospital. All the way down Country Club Road, she looked for the girl. Disappointment at not seeing her near the campus gave way to relief as she spied her standing nervously on the other side of the road.

On her way home, Joyce felt an even stronger impulse to stop. As she approached the girl, Joyce felt her foot leave the gas pedal and reach for the brake. At the last second, though, she accelerated, whispering under her breath, "No, I am not going to get involved. We already have enough burdens at The Lighthouse. I had better not get involved again."

Just before four o'clock, Joyce's father pulled

into the driveway. "Joyce," he asked, "could you please take me to the hospital to see your mother? The parking situation there is terrible, and I was wondering if you could drop me off and then pick me up at five o'clock?"

"Sure, Daddy," Joyce said. "I'll be glad to take you." In the back of Joyce's mind, she was still curious about the girl. As she passed by the campus, she spotted the girl, still standing along the road, looking lonely and perplexed and methodically watching the traffic.

When Joyce returned for her father, her eyes again searched the road, hoping to see her "friend." If the girl was still standing there on her trip back home, Joyce knew she had to stop and speak with her. Sure enough, she was still there.

Joyce's father stood waiting as she drove up to the entrance of the hospital. As he got into the car, she instructed him, "Daddy, when we go down Country Club Road, I want you to tell me what you think of a girl standing near the college campus. I have passed her seven times today during my trips back and forth to the hospital."

As they approached the girl, the urge to stop became unbearable. Just as Joyce began to brake, her father said, "Keep going. She looks like a little tramp!"

Her father's words quenched the urge to stop that had been germinating in Joyce all day. It was replaced by a sickening feeling. "She looks like a little tramp!" kept ringing through her head, piercing her heart.

On their arrival back home, Morgan came out to greet them. Joyce's father got out of the car, but Joyce did not. "I'll be right back!" she said, putting the car in reverse and backing out of the driveway.

Joyce found this trip difficult. Immediately she began to pray, "Forgive me, Jesus, for now I know it was You who wanted me to stop. Forgive me for my disobedience to Your leading." How ashamed she felt for not wanting to get involved. Joyce knew she had to find that girl or else spend a night without sleep.

Anxiously, Joyce searched both sides of the road. But this time there was no sign of the girl. She had vanished. Joyce's heart sank, and she began praying frantically. "Jesus, please help me find her, because I know You want me to do something for her."

Turning the car around at the nearest gas station, Joyce stopped and looked in all directions. Nothing! Then she happened to look inside the gas station. There sat the girl, talking to the attendant. Joyce uttered a cry of delight and a "Thank You" to God.

With a look of surprise, the girl responded to Joyce's invitation to come to the car. When Joyce opened the door and got out to greet her, the girl responded angrily, "What do you want?"

"Do you need help?" Joyce asked.

"What's it to you?" she snapped back defensively.

"Come on now!" Joyce replied. "I have seen you eight times today. I know you need help. It's getting dark, and I can see you are cold. If you need it, I'm here to help you."

After pausing a second, Joyce looked directly into her eyes and added, "Anyhow, Jesus sent me to help you."

The girl's eyes suddenly filled with tears. Through her sobs she confessed, "You probably won't believe this, but as I walked down the road today I cried to God. I told Him, 'If You are real, You had better send someone to help me.'"

"Four years ago, at age 17, I ran away from home," she continued. "Four days ago, I left Lighthouse Point, Florida, with a truck driver with whom I've been living. He promised to take care of me and take me along with him in his rig. He dropped me off at this corner, telling me he had to get gas. He promised to come right back. He never did. Everything I own is still in his truck."

"Come on," Joyce urged, opening the passenger's door of the car. "I live just up the road. It's supper time and everything is ready."

The girl got into the car, and Joyce headed home. "What's your name?" she asked after a few minutes.

"Wendy," the girl responded, "What's yours?"

"Joyce."

Morgan and Joyce's father were still standing in the driveway. As Joyce and Wendy got out of the car, Joyce's father remarked to Morgan, "I told you so!" He knew Joyce had gone back for the girl by the side of the road.

Soon everyone gathered around the supper table, holding hands in prayer. Morgan led, "Jesus, You know there's a real need at this table tonight. We ask You to meet that need."

Silence fell on the table as everyone, including Morgan, began to cry. After Morgan's "Amen," Joyce looked over at her father. Tears filled his eyes.

Wendy did not eat much, and after a few moments she excused herself, went into the living room and began to sob quietly. Joyce was about to get up to go and comfort Wendy, when her father rose from his seat and walked into the living room. He sat down beside the "little tramp" and placed his arm around her.

"Everything is going to work out," he said. "I don't know what you've been through, but it will work out."

Later that evening, sitting in Claude's old bedroom, Joyce began to talk with Wendy. "You know, God has a plan for your life. He really did bring you here. I was 32 years old when God revealed His plan for my life. Here you are only 21. You have years ahead of you."

"What do I have to do?" Wendy asked.

"Allow Jesus to come into your heart!" Joyce replied.

Wendy then prayed, asking Jesus to forgive her sins and to come and live in her heart—and God answered. The two women embraced, warm tears of joy streaming down both of their cheeks. After several moments of silence, Wendy looked at Joyce and said, "You know what? My mother and grandmother have been praying for me for four years."

Joyce could not help recalling God's promise in Acts 16:31, "Believe in the Lord Jesus, and you will be saved—you and your household."

"Why don't we call someone in your family and tell them about this?" Joyce asked. Joyce picked up the telephone, asking Wendy for a phone number. Wendy gave Joyce her sister's telephone number in Williamsport, Pennsylvania.

Wendy's sister was overjoyed to hear from her and immediately requested that Wendy come to her house on the first available bus. After hanging up, Joyce called the depot and found that the bus left at nine o'clock the next morning.

When things settled down and Wendy was in bed, Joyce had time to reflect back over the day's events. She praised God for allowing her to meet Wendy and lead her to Christ. Suddenly she wondered, "What is Wendy going to wear home tomorrow? My clothes will never fit her tiny frame!"

Trying to think of someone who might have clothes to fit Wendy, a name came into Joyce's mind—Nancy Braun, the assistant pastor's wife. She called immediately and explained the situation. "Nancy, would you possibly have an old pair of shoes and an old dress and coat we could have?" Nancy promised to look and have her husband, Paul, deliver them the next morning.

Early the next morning, Pastor Paul arrived with the promised articles of clothing. When Wendy tried them on, they fit perfectly. "When the Lord does something, He does it right!" she exclaimed.

During the trip to the bus terminal, Joyce played the car radio. "Today is Columbus Day," the announcer remarked. "On this day in 1492 Columbus discovered the New World." Wendy cheerfully added, "And today I discovered my new life!"

From that point, things happened quickly. The bus sat ready for departure, and Joyce had to hurry and purchase Wendy's ticket. They exchanged farewell hugs, and Wendy left.

Coming home in the car, eyes welling with tears, Joyce felt a real communion with her Lord. "Joyce, you were obedient," God seemed to be saying. "All this would not have been possible if you had not stopped."

How humble Joyce felt, yet how uplifted. Then she remembered Psalm 119:2, "Blessed are they who keep his statutes and seek him with all their heart."

Three days later Joyce and Morgan received a nice thank-you note and reimbursement for the bus ticket. Since then, they had not heard from Wendy until the telephone call. How the Lord worked!

CHAPTER
17

The Men of the House

ALONG WITH THE MANY mothers-to-be and other young women who came to The Lighthouse, there were also a number of young men. Most were college students studying at York College, but some were just individuals needing special love and attention.

Butch was the first of the single male residents, and he came in December 1975, soon after Claude's death. He was finishing his college work at Penn State University and was in York to do his student teaching. He had a contact through the Alliance church, and Joyce and Morgan agreed to let him stay at The Lighthouse during this three-month term.

Butch never complained, even though he was shuffled from room to room to make space for newcomers. He played the guitar, and soon found himself teaching Amy basic chords. He even helped her compose her first original song.

One day he approached Joyce. "Someday I hope I'm going to be married," he confessed. "Thinking about it, though, frightens me. I don't know what kind of a position a man should take in the home." By the time he left The Lighthouse,

91

though, he was confident. He told Joyce, "In watching Morgan I have learned how a Christian man should act as head of his home. He needs to be tough, but gentle!"

The next young man who stayed at The Lighthouse came in the fall of 1976. Joyce received a call one day from a stranger who gave the name of one of the girls who had lived with them. He indicated that he was stranded and wondered if he could stay at The Lighthouse overnight. When Joyce picked him up at the bus station, all of his possessions were in a paper bag. He told Joyce that he had lost his luggage at the bus terminal in Harrisburg. As soon as Morgan met him and heard his story, he sensed something was not right. That night in bed, Morgan told Joyce, "This young man needs help, but he's not being truthful with us."

The "overnight" stay extended into a week, and Bill soon confessed that he had not lost his baggage and that he was not really stranded. He had run away from home and needed a place to stay. All he had in the world was what he brought in the paper bag.

Because of an uneasy feeling about Bill, Morgan decided to put a limit on his stay. "We're going to allow you to live here for three weeks," Morgan told him. "At the end of those three weeks, that's it! We'll help you find a job, but whatever happens, three weeks is your limit here. Do you understand?"

"Yes," he replied.

The first problem arose soon into the first week. Morgan, with his customary generosity, told Bill to raid the refrigerator when he wanted. Bill, however, overdid it. No sooner was dinner over, than Bill was in the refrigerator hunting for something to eat! Morgan sensed that Bill did not really have a notion of proper conduct. So he had a talk with him, and Bill seemed to understand.

Before the three weeks were up, Bill got a job and was able to move into an apartment with four other Christian young men. The situation seemed promising for Bill, but it quickly unraveled. He would not pull his weight around the apartment or at his job, which he quickly lost.

Soon Bill was back at The Lighthouse, asking Morgan what he should do. "Well," Morgan started, "I'm going to be honest with you. You're like bad money. You're just a 'sponger.' Nobody wants you around because you won't pull your own weight, and you take advantage of people. You know that you brought all this on yourself. We gave you a chance from the beginning and tried to help you, but you took advantage of us. You're going to have to learn to grow up or you'll have trouble the rest of your life. My suggestion is—and I'm telling you just like I would tell my own son—to buy a bus ticket and go back where you came from. It's no better here than there, because you're still the same person. The best thing for you to do is to go home and straighten out your life there. Maybe then you will be ready for something new."

These were hard words, but they were words Bill needed to hear. No one had ever talked with him like that. Soon Bill left. Since then he has settled down, married and even adopted a son.

In 1978, The Lighthouse became home to a York College student. Jim was a dedicated student, and he knew where he was going—he wanted to be a doctor. Jim had a problem, though. He had trouble relating to and interacting with people.

The Lighthouse, with its constant influx of people, proved to be the perfect environment for improving his relational skills. Jim and Joyce would often stay up until one or two o'clock in the morning talking. After a short time, he became an integral part of the household, developing close relationships unlike any he had previously experienced.

Joe and Rod, two other college students, arrived at The Lighthouse in the fall of 1979. Joe came orginally from a small town not far from York, although he had recently been living in California. He was hitchhiking, and a man from the Ilgenfritzes' church picked him up. This man talked to him and invited him to church. The assistant pastor took him under his wing and eventually led him to the Lord. When Joe explained that he was enrolled in York College for the fall semester but that he did not have money to afford housing, he expressed to the assistant pastor his need for a place to live. The pastor immediately thought of The Lighthouse and gave Joyce a call. The Ilgenfritzes accepted, and Joe moved in.

If Joe was anything, he was honest—honest to the point of saying what he thought to anyone. If he saw something in a person that he disliked, he would tell that person. No one knew what he might say next.

As would be expected, this honesty brought conflicts—something Amy soon found out! Joe reminded her of Butch in many ways, and Butch had been her special friend. One night Joe asked Amy if he could talk with her. She readily complied. "Amy," he began, "I want to tell you something. I don't really like you. I think you're a phony and that you're on a giant ego trip!"

Amy did not know what to say. She was both crushed and dumbfounded. No one had ever spoken to her like that.

Because of his free-spirited life in California, Joe had acquired some other unique traits. He immediately took an interest in the kitchen and food preparation. He believed in eating only natural foods, and soon had Joyce and the rest of the household thinking—and eating—the same way.

Yet Joe, too, was searching for direction and purpose to his life. He gave the appearance of knowing what he wanted to do and where he was going. The longer he lived at The Lighthouse, however, the more Joyce and Morgan sensed that this was not really the case.

One night he and Morgan started talking. Morgan could tell that some of the goals he had set for himself were unrealistic and that, to some extent, he was living in a fantasy world. "Why don't you make a list of those goals that you're sure are within your reach?" Morgan suggested. "Then, as you attain those, it will give you confidence to attempt something bigger."

Rooming with Joe was Rod—his complete opposite in every respect. Joe was a leader. Rod was a follower. Joe had a sense of which way his life was headed. Rod had no idea what he wanted to do.

Rod came from a home environment characterized by instability. His father died when he was young, and even though his mother was a Christian and made sure that he went to church and Sunday school, Rod rejected the whole idea of Christianity. His brother contracted muscular dystrophy, and because Rod feared that he, too, might succumb to the disease, he constantly worked out with weights.

Before moving into The Lighthouse, Rod had his own apartment, but it proved to be too much for him to handle financially. Looking at the campus bulletin board one day, he noticed an advertisement for the York Christian and Missionary Alliance Church and decided to attend the next Sunday. As he walked into the sanctuary that Sunday morning, he told the usher he was a college student. The usher then seated him beside Joyce and Morgan. As they conversed, Rod mentioned that he was seeking another place to live. With that, Joyce invited him for dinner. That afternoon, he moved into The Lighthouse.

Rod was a follower. One of his friends, Jim, attended church with him. Jim had a peculiar habit—he never wore socks to church. One Sunday morning, before leaving for church, Joyce noticed Rod's feet. "Rod, come on!" Joyce exclaimed, "Where are your socks?"

"Jim doesn't wear socks," he replied sheepishly.

On another occasion, Amy and Beth reported to Joyce that Rod planned to have his ear pierced because one of his friends had had his pierced. He even had the earring on his dresser.

Joyce stalked to his room. "What's this I hear about an earring?" she asked. Seating herself, she put her opened Bible on her lap, and said, "Let me share some Scripture with you."

> Therefore, I urge you, brothers, in view of God's mercy, to offer your bodies as living sacrifices, holy and pleasing to God—which is your spiritual worship. Do not conform any longer to the pattern of this world, but be transformed by the renewing of your mind. Then you will be able to test and approve what God's will is—his good, pleasing and perfect will (Romans 12:1–2).

"Do you mean that if I got an earring, I wouldn't be accepted in your church?"

"No, that's not it at all," Joyce answered. "God wants us to give our bodies to Him as a sacrifice, pleasing to Him. Do you think it will please Him if you wear an earring, Rod? Think about it. Why do you want to be identified with guys who have earrings?"

The discussion continued for some time before Rod finally decided that what Joyce was saying made sense.

While Rod and Joe were different, they also complemented each other. Rod wanted to be a ladies' man, but he really was not. He had the muscles, but not the technique. Joe had the technique. So the two of them together fared quite well.

Both of these young men—as did the others—came to The Lighthouse with some sort of problem and with nothing of substance in their lives. Once they found that they could trust the Lord—and after seeing real faith lived out in the lives of the Ilgenfritzes—a real change came over them. A letter written by Rod soon after leaving The Lighthouse sums up the impact this family had on the lives of these young men.

Dear Family:

Since leaving The Lighthouse, I have had quite a number of opportunities to share my testimony. I tell people about the family in Pennsylvania who let me live in their home, showing me—not just telling me—how a Christian should live.

As you well know, I learned some important lessons that year in Pennsylvania. Most important was to realize the impact—good or bad—that we can have on others just by our everyday actions. Because of this, I also learned that we need to always be careful to show love and concern. The right response to the situations and people that come across our paths is important.

I am back in school now, majoring in rehabilitation therapy and trusting God to lead me. Thanks again for everything!

Love,

Rod

CHAPTER
18

Do We Need Another Son?

ANOTHER SPECIAL YOUNG MAN who came to live at The Lighthouse was a 16-year-old named Dwayne. He had been recommended to The Lighthouse by Pastor John Oldfield—a personal friend of the Ilgenfritzes and pastor of the Yorktown Chapel. Dwayne was a delinquent youth who had been expelled from high school during his sophomore year because of his constant fighting. He was now working as a dishwasher at the York Hospital.

During Pastor Oldfield's conversation with Joyce about Dwayne, he told her, "Even though he has been drinking and getting into all kinds of trouble, I still see much potential in him. He helps me around the church with chores and is, overall, a good, but misdirected, teenager. What he needs is direction. I think you and Morgan would be perfect for him."

"I don't know, Pastor," Joyce answered. "We have two pregnant girls with us now who are about to have their babies. I don't think we can handle a rebellious 16-year-old boy just now."

"OK," Pastor Oldfield said, "but I wish you would talk to Morgan about it."

Several days later, Pastor Oldfield telephoned Joyce to see if she had talked to Morgan.

"No, I haven't," Joyce confessed.

Just then, Morgan came through the door. "Hold on, Pastor, Morgan just came home. Let me see what he says."

After Morgan had been briefed on the Pastor's proposal, he replied, "All I can say is to have the pastor bring the boy out here so we can at least meet him." Joyce relayed this message to Pastor Oldfield, and a time was arranged the following Sunday afternoon for the meeting.

That Sunday morning in their own church, Joyce and Morgan heard a sermon entitled, "Be Willing to Say Yes to Jesus." Joyce and Morgan looked at each other and somehow knew that Dwayne would be staying.

They went out for dinner after church, and when they arrived home, they found the pastor and Dwayne waiting for them.

After introductions and some chitchat, Morgan looked directly at Dwayne and said, "Well, son, we will try it for two weeks and see what happens, but you are going to have to do things our way. Drinking, drugs and smoking are not allowed."

"Yes sir!" Dwayne said.

About this time, the Ilgenfritzes' youngest daughter, Beth, bounced into the living room. Spotting Dwayne, she said, "Is he going to live here?"

"Yes," Joyce replied.

"Good!" she exclaimed.

That seemed to break the ice, and Dwayne smiled.

"I guess you can send over his things," Morgan commented.

"That won't be necessary," Pastor Oldfield replied. "They are already in the car. Dwayne, why don't you bring them into the house?"

At first, Dwayne reacted to everything in a high-strung, nervous manner. One night soon after he moved into The Lighthouse, he rode his bicycle over to his girlfriend's house and stayed out until late that night. When he returned, he found Morgan at the door waiting for him. Morgan ushered him into the house by the collar. "Young man, this is the last time you are going to hop on your bike without telling us where you are going!" Morgan said in an authoritative voice. "And, you will not be allowed to stay out until all hours of the night. Do you understand?"

"Yes," Dwayne replied quickly.

After several more confrontations, Dwayne began to adapt to his new family and their rules. He also began to notice a difference between his life and the Ilgenfritzes'. He saw Mark Ilgenfritz having fun during his senior year in high school. Dwayne spent his days working in the hospital kitchen.

One day he told Joyce, "I wish I could be like Mark and Amy."

"You can," Joyce assured him. "But you will have to go back to school."

"I can't go back to school," Dwayne said. "They won't let me back in because of my fighting."

"If you are really serious about this," Joyce said, "we will see what we can do. Maybe the Christian school where Mark and Amy go will accept you."

Because of their tight finances, Joyce knew they could not afford to pay Dwayne's tuition. She decided to pray about it. She somehow felt that God would provide a way if He wanted Dwayne to return to school.

The next day, Beth and Joyce went to a Chinese restaurant for lunch. While seated at their table, Beth began a conversation with an elderly lady at the next table.

"You know," the lady told Joyce, "I just love children. I was a first-grade teacher for 30 years."

"How would you like a ride home," Joyce offered.

"I would love to go along with my lovely little friend here," the lady said.

In the car, Beth decided to give her an invitation as only a little girl could, "Would you like to come to my house to see my pet skunk?"

"Not a pet skunk? Wow!" the woman said, slightly surprised. "I would be *delighted* to see your pet skunk."

At home, Joyce began telling her about the whole family. She played a tape of Amy singing one of her own original compositions called "Friends." While listening to the tape, the lady began to cry. "That was beautiful," she said at its conclusion.

Somehow, the subject changed to Dwayne. Joyce explained why he was there and about his desire to return to school. Then she drove the lady home.

One morning a few days after this, Joyce felt burdened about the school situation. She drove to her church so she could pray at the altar on Dwayne's behalf. Pastor Muir met her at the door and asked if he could help. She explained the situation to him, and together they prayed that the Lord would provide the needed money.

When Joyce returned home, she noticed a note on the refrigerator door asking her to call a certain number. She dialed the number and to her surprise, she heard the voice of the retired teacher she had met in the Chinese restaurant. "I have been thinking about that boy all day," the woman began. "I would like to help him go to that Christian school, but I can't do it by myself. My neighbor is wealthy, and I am going next door to talk to her. I will offer to pay half of his tuition if she will pay the other half."

Soon the lady called back with good news: Dwayne's tuition would be taken care of. Joyce rejoiced and praised the Lord for this answer to prayer. When she told Dwayne, he could not understand why complete strangers would pay his way to school, and Joyce used this opportunity to witness to him of God's faithfulness in answering prayer.

Joyce called the school and made an appointment with the principal. Sitting in his office, Joyce and Dwayne listened carefully to what the principal said. "Young man, there is one thing we are *not* looking for around here, and that is another discipline problem."

"I promise," Dwayne answered quickly, "I will not be a problem."

After the interview, the principal informed them that the school would do its best to try and have him finish 10th grade that year.

On Dwayne's first day, Morgan gave him some fatherly advice. "Son, keep those fists down!"

Somehow, though, Dwayne's reputation preceded him, and he became the target of some boys who were willing to test him. Dwayne did not give in and fight, though; he kept his promise.

The turning point of Dwayne's life came at midnight one day in May when he received Jesus into his heart. Nothing drastic happened right away, but a constant growth and a real turning away from his old life was evident after that decision. He passed 10th grade and was allowed to continue school the next year. During 11th grade, he made the basketball and soccer teams. By his senior year, Dwayne became the soccer team's leading scorer. This boy who had never participated in organized sports now excelled in this area. His academic progress was also amazing; he had always been just an average student.

At his class's commencement, Dwayne's peers recognized him as the student who had most improved. Because of this honor, he had the opportunity to share what Jesus had done in his life before the entire audience.

What an occasion! Here stood a young man who just a few years earlier appeared to be headed nowhere. His family had given up on him. Now he stood as a glowing testimony to God's grace. As he told about how Jesus had changed his life and about the family who shared the love of Jesus with him, Joyce and Morgan started to cry. Inwardly, they thanked Jesus for what He had done and for Dwayne—their "second son."

CHAPTER

19

A Living Gospel

THE CONSTANT FLOW of people who stayed as temporary or longer-term guests at The Lighthouse naturally made for stressful situations. Were it not for the Lord and the discipline of daily Bible reading and prayer, Joyce and Morgan could not have survived. Through daily living they discovered the relevance of the Bible that had become an integral part of their life.

One wintry day Joyce sat in the doctor's waiting room as Morgan was being examined for an illness. She noticed a Bible on the end table, picked it up and began reading from Matthew.

> Then the King will say to those on his right, "Come, you who are blessed by my Father; take your inheritance, the kingdom prepared for you since the creation of the world. For I was hungry and you gave me something to eat, I was thirsty and you gave me something to drink, I was a stranger and you invited me in, I needed clothes and you clothed me, I was sick and you looked after me, I was in prison and you came to visit me."
>
> Then the righteous will answer him, "Lord, when did we see you hungry and feed you, or thirsty and give you something to drink? When did we see you a stranger and invite

you in, or needing clothes and clothe you? When did we see you sick or in prison and go to visit you?"

The King will reply, "I tell you the truth, whatever you did for one of the least of these brothers of mine, you did for me."

Closing the Bible, Joyce began to think. *Had not she and Morgan been faithful in doing this? Surely all the people who had come to live at The Lighthouse would qualify as those in need.* Then something seemed to come to her mind, and she felt convicted. "Lord," she prayed silently, "show me what these verses *really* mean. I want to know the depths of this passage."

Returning home, Joyce followed the doctor's instructions and put Morgan to bed. He was running a 104 degree temperature. About 3:30 in the morning, half-asleep, Joyce heard the doorbell ring. Normally at that time of the night Morgan would answer it, but because of his illness, Joyce went to the door. She opened the door as far as the safety chain allowed and peeked out into the darkness. The cold winter air blasted snow through the crack. There, to one side, was the figure of an old man, shivering.

"Let me in!" his frail voice pleaded.

"Where are you going?" Joyce asked.

"Let me in, my feet are cold!" he continued.

Joyce looked down and saw that he wore no shoes, then quickly searched his wrist for a hospital bracelet but found none. After inviting him inside, she soaked his feet in warm water as he tried to explain his situation.

With his feet warming in the basin of water, his

body wrapped securely in a blanket and his stomach full of warm milk, he looked around the kitchen and said, "I like it here. I think I will stay!"

Morgan soon appeared in a half-conscious state at the top of the steps, wondering why Joyce had not returned to bed. Upon hearing her explanation, he suggested she call the police. They confirmed the report of a man missing from a nearby nursing home.

Soon, two police officers arrived at the Ilgenfritz house and volunteered to escort the elderly man back to the nursing home. As they were about to leave, one officer turned to Joyce and said, "Out of all the houses on this street, I wonder why he chose yours?"

After they were gone, Joyce remembered the Scripture she had read earlier that day in the doctor's office and her prayer asking the Lord to make that Scripture real. She walked to the sofa, dropped to her knees and began worshiping Jesus, thanking Him for answering her prayer.

CHAPTER

20

Our New Son Is an Uncle!

AFTER SEVERAL YEARS of taking in people, the Ilgenfritzes were accustomed to unusual events. They knew the Lord often worked in strange ways, but there were still occasional surprises.

One of these came on a winter night in February 1981. The family had just sat down to dinner, when the doorbell rang. Upon opening the door, Joyce discovered a boy standing in the doorway with a newspaper clipping in his hand.

"Does Dwayne live here?" he asked.

"Yes," Joyce said, curious.

"My name is Danny," he said, "and Dwayne is my uncle."

Joyce invited him in and called for Dwayne. When Dwayne appeared, he looked puzzled for a moment.

"Dwayne, don't you know me?" Danny asked. "It's me, Danny!"

"Danny!" Dwayne said. "I didn't recognize you. You're so skinny."

"Look what I cut out of the newspaper," Danny boasted, holding up the clipping for Dwayne to see. At the end of the soccer season, there had been an article in the local newspaper about Dwayne's soccer team. Accompanying the article was a photograph of Dwayne. "You are a soccer star," Danny continued. "The last time I saw you, you were a dope addict!"

Dwayne did not quite know what to say, and the two boys stood looking at each other for a moment. Joyce suggested Dwayne give Danny a hug, and he did.

"I came to see if you had any clothes I could wear," Danny said. "I just ran away from home. I got tired of this," he said as he lifted his shirt exposing huge, red welts across his back. "I went to Grandma's house, and she told me to come here to see you about some clothes. Do think you could find me some, Dwayne?"

"Sure, come on upstairs," Dwayne told him.

Downstairs, dinner waiting, Joyce plopped down on the sofa with tears in her eyes. The Lord had brought another "stranger" to her door.

When the two returned, Joyce suggested that Danny stay for dinner. At the table, Danny sat beside Dwayne. As they held hands and bowed their heads for prayer—something new for Danny—he continued to hold the clipping in his hand. Everyone was touched.

It was prayer meeting night, and after dinner, Joyce and Morgan prepared to go. When they returned home, they found Danny asleep upstairs in Dwayne's bed. Just like a mother hen, Dwayne told them to be quiet and not wake him. He ended up staying the night.

The next morning Danny came downstairs and cuddled up next to Joyce on the sofa. "God answered a prayer last night," he said. "Dwayne

prayed that I would not have any more night-
mares, and last night I didn't have any. Do you
think He might answer another one?" he asked
Joyce.

"What is that?" Joyce asked cautiously,
already learning that Danny was something of a
manipulator.

"That I could come to live here with you and
Dwayne," he quickly replied.

Without waiting for a reply, he added, "I am
also praying for a large print Bible to read. My
eyes are bad, and it's hard for me to read."

"I don't know about the first request," Joyce
told him, "but I have a Bible you can have."

After giving him the Bible, Joyce continued her
morning chores. She was supposed to attend a
Bible study and had to get ready. "I am going to a
Bible study this morning, and I will drop you off
at your grandmother's house on the way," she
told Danny.

"Bible study!" Danny chirped, "I have never
been to a Bible study. Could I come with you?"

Unsure of what to do, Joyce finally consented.
She could take him to his grandmother's after the
meeting. Although determined to be rid of him,
deep inside Joyce knew he would probably end
up at The Lighthouse.

When they arrived at the Bible study, the other
women did not quite know what to think about
the little boy with long hair and too-big clothes.
They doted on him, and he turned on the charm.
He immediately sat down next to the leader.
When she asked the group the question, "What
does it mean to be crucified with Christ?"
Danny's hand shot up.

"Yes, Danny?" the leader asked, "What do you think it means?"

"I think that being crucified with Christ means that when you get beaten, and Christ is in you, then He is getting beaten too." The women were silent after that answer, most of them trying to hold back the tears.

During prayer time, Danny prayed, "Lord, You have answered so many prayers. You know I want to come and live with the Ilgenfritz family. I have one more request, though, could you give me a bicycle?"

The next week those women took an offering and bought Danny a bicycle!

Driving home—with Danny—Joyce prayed silently, "Lord, I cannot make an intelligent decision about this whole matter. I am too emotionally involved. I know Danny needs a home, but at this point I really don't want him because I know what that will involve. You know that I cannot say no to You. The only way I know that I will be able to hear from You about Danny is to be submissive to Morgan. Whatever Morgan says, I will take for Your answer."

That afternoon Danny's caseworker visited The Lighthouse. After talking with Danny in private, she came downstairs in tears. "That boy is too good to be true," she told Joyce.

While the caseworker was still conversing with Joyce, Morgan came home from work. Joyce introduced him to Danny's caseworker, and they talked for a while. Finally the caseworker told them, "I have just been to see Danny's mother. She says she never wants to see him again. I have got to find a home for this boy."

"I have not had the chance to discuss this with my wife," Morgan replied, "but I could not even eat my lunch today thinking about this boy. I really do not want an 11-year-old boy at this time in my life, but we have said, 'Yes, Lord.' How can I say no when a boy needs a home? If my wife is in agreement, we will take Danny."

The answer had come through Morgan just as Joyce had prayed. Two weeks later they became Danny's legal guardians.

CHAPTER
21

Stranded!

Part of Joyce's summer routine each year was working as camp nurse at Summit Grove Camp, a Christian and Missionary Alliance camp located south of York in New Freedom, Pennsylvania. The middle Saturday of camp was always designated as Family Day, and this day usually brought in the largest crowd. During the summer of 1980, a large group of more than 100 Hmong refugees were in attendance. While watching them eat their picnic lunch of oriental food, Joyce felt a warmth and a compassion for them.

Then one of their children fell and cut his leg, and his parents brought him to Joyce for treatment. Joyce met the parents and some other relatives, and an immediate bond of friendship developed.

During the service that night, Joyce could think of nothing but the Hmong people. God was speaking to her, she knew, preparing her for something new. She was so caught up with these individuals that she even dreamed about them that night.

Sunday afternoon after church, Joyce and Morgan decided to relax and rest. Joyce could not get comfortable on the camper bed, though. Suddenly she turned to Morgan and said, "Honey, let's drive home this afternoon.

"We'll be going home in just a few days," Morgan grumbled, not wanting to make the drive home.

"I know," Joyce added, "but I have this urge to go home. Maybe the dog needs water."

"If you want to go home, you can go," Morgan sighed. "I'm tired and I am going to stay here and rest. I won't feel bad if you want to take a ride. Go ahead."

That was all Joyce needed to hear. In no time, she was out of the camp and on Interstate 83 heading home. After only a short distance, she noticed a man ahead waving a white handkerchief. Her foot immediately went to the brake pedal, and she pulled off the road.

Seven Oriental people ran over to her car at once, all talking in their native tongue and motioning to their car, indicating that something was wrong. Joyce could not understand a word they said. Then, one young woman spoke to her in fluent English. She informed Joyce that she was from France, and these were her relatives from Lebanon, Pennsylvania. The group was returning from a trip to Washington, D.C., where they had visited another relative. They had been sitting on the side of the road in the sweltering heat for two hours, and no one had stopped to help them.

"Get the driver and come with me," Joyce told the young woman, "and I will take you to a service station." The service station dispatched a tow truck. After analyzing the problem, the mechanic said it was serious and would take several days to repair. He hooked up the car to the tow truck and drove off, leaving the seven Vietnamese standing by the road.

Joyce looked at them, then toward heaven. Meeting the Hmong people at camp on Saturday now came to her mind. The Lord had prepared her for this situation and had brought her to help them. She loaded them all in her car and headed home.

Because Joyce and Morgan had been away for two weeks, there was very little food in the house, but Joyce managed to find something for them to eat, serving it with lemonade. Soon everyone was having a great time.

The one young woman became Joyce's interpreter. She worked for the Laotian Embassy in France and could speak five languages fluently. After a while, Joyce told her, "I believe God sent me to help you and your family."

She translated this for her relatives, "God . . . sent . . . her . . . to . . . help . . . us." They all responded by nodding their heads in acknowledgement.

"Do you know that God has a plan for your life?" Joyce continued. "I know He does, because He made me come to your aid. Part of His plan for you is that you learn about Him," Joyce shared through her interpreter.

They talked for a short time, then asked if they could use her phone. They called one of their relatives in Lebanon who agreed to come for them. About 10:00 P.M. that night, he arrived. As they stood in the driveway preparing to leave, Joyce asked them all to make a big circle and hold hands, and she led in prayer.

"Thank You, Lord, for bringing this precious family to The Lighthouse. Thank You also for helping me to be sensitive to Your leading. Go with this family, now, and bring someone else across their path to tell them more about You. Amen."

After the prayer, they all thanked Joyce, piled into the car and left.

As the car pulled away, Joyce lifted her head toward heaven and breathed a prayer of thanks to God for alerting her to this needy family. Once again, God had brought strangers to her door!

CHAPTER

22

The Far East Comes to The Lighthouse

BECAUSE OF JOYCE'S contacts with Orientals, God caused a love for them to grow in her heart. She promised God to be available to Him and prayed that He would let her win some of them to Christ.

God answered Joyce's prayers when The Lighthouse's first Oriental guest, a native Japanese girl named Junko, arrived in the spring of 1981.

Junko had come to America the year before and had lived with a woman in Lancaster for the summer. This woman was a Christian and eventually led Junko to the Lord. Junko later moved to York to attend York College. Her first place of residence in York was with an elderly woman. This woman became seriously ill, however, and she was placed in a nursing home. Junko was left without a place to live. This lady's pastor, however, knew of the Ilgenfritzes' ministry and contacted them, asking if Junko might live with them. Joyce immediately sensed it was the Lord's leading and, of course, agreed.

Junko soon became a part of the Ilgenfritz family, and they affectionately called her their Japanese Princess. She spent a year and a half at The Lighthouse while she attended York College.

Amy Ilgenfritz and Junko became good friends. They spent the whole summer together before Amy returned to Bible college. During the summer, Amy discipled Junko on a one-to-one basis, encouraging her to read and study God's Word.

When Amy returned to college, a person would have thought the two were sisters by the tears they shed. Whenever a letter arrived from her, Junko would also share in the family's joy.

One day shortly after Amy left, Junko said to Joyce, "After experiencing Amy's departure and seeing how you and Morgan miss her, I know how my mother felt when I left Japan to come to America." Because of these feelings, she wrote a beautiful letter to her mother in Japan telling her how much she missed her and that she loved her very much.

That summer Amy and Junko engaged in many long talks about Christianity. With Amy's encouragement, Junko decided to remain in the States an additional six months to take classes at Lancaster Bible College. There she would receive the necessary Bible training to help her witness to those in her home country. During those six months, she returned to the Ilgenfritz home on weekends.

Through Junko, Hing, a Chinese student, became another special Oriental friend at The Lighthouse. Although she did not live at The Lighthouse—she lived in an apartment across the street—she became a regular visitor. Because she was close to her family, who had worked hard to send her to America, Hing battled with periods of depression and homesickness. She found love and concern at The Lighthouse, and the Ilgenfritzes became her American family.

Junko had a Japanese friend, Keichi, who spent time with her. They would speak in Japanese and talk about Japan. This helped Junko to not feel so far away from home. Her friend soon left to return to Tokyo, though, and Junko was disappointed to see him leave. Right after he left, Joyce and Morgan prayed with Junko that the Lord would send her another Japanese friend.

The very next day, Hing came in from school beaming. "Joyce, Junko, I have exciting news! A new Japanese girl is on campus. She just arrived. Can we invite her to dinner?"

The next evening, the new girl, Keiko (Kay e ko), had dinner with the Ilgenfritz family. After the meal, with Junko translating, Keiko shared what had happened to her upon her arrival in America. After landing in Bridgeport, Connecticut, she took a taxi to the bus station. There, three men assaulted her, taking her purse which contained her passport, traveler's checks and cash. She could not even tell the police what had happened because she did not know enough English. They arranged for a hotel room for her until the next day, when she could get her traveler's checks replaced. Sitting on her bed that night, she broke down and cried, feeling like she should return to Japan. She suddenly hated America.

The Ilgenfritzes were the first American family she actually met, and after spending time with them, her initial judgment of America changed.

As they accepted her into their household, she became another Ilgenfritz family member. During school breaks such as Christmas and Easter, when everyone else went home, she came to The Lighthouse to stay.

Just before her graduation from York College, Junko received a letter from a friend in Japan who said that she wanted to come to the United States to visit an American family. Junko relayed this request to Joyce, asking if she and the girl could both stay at The Lighthouse. This would be during Junko's last month at Bible college. Both girls then planned to return to Japan together. Junko truly believed that if her friend stayed at The Lighthouse, she would learn about Jesus and accept Him as her Savior. Because Joyce and Morgan had had such a good experience with Junko and Keiko, this proposal sounded exciting!

That next year, right after Easter, Junko's friend, Motoko, arrived. "Good morning," "Hello" and "Thank you" were the extent of her knowledge of English. Everywhere she went, she carried her little Japanese/English dictionary.

Motoko wanted to learn everything she could about American life and customs. She spent much of her time watching and helping Joyce make meals and do chores. Through these times of working together and sharing through broken English, Joyce and Motoko came to really love one another.

Motoko had learned flower arranging in Japan. One day, Joyce invited her to a women's meeting to hear a Christian woman talk about flower arranging. Although Joyce did not tell Motoko, the speaker used flower arranging as a way to present the gospel.

Before this woman's presentation, Motoko excused herself to go to the rest room. While she was out, the president of the group asked for prayer requests. Joyce requested that they pray for the Holy Spirit to help Motoko understand what was about to be said. As everyone began praying, Motoko returned, not knowing that they were praying for her.

The speaker began her presentation by producing a basket arrangement. "Just like this arrangement," she said, "God has a perfect design for your life." As she talked, Joyce wrote down key words like "design" while Motoko looked them up in her dictionary. Then she would acknowledge to Joyce that she understood.

Next, the speaker placed several thistles and pine cones in the arrangement. "This symbolizes how sin in our lives distorts that perfect design," she said. In conclusion, she placed red flowers in the design, explaining how Jesus shed His blood, dying on the cross for the sins of the world. "His blood removes our sins," she finished, as she removed the undesirable weeds. It was an eloquent picture, and Motoko seemed to understand it all!

The night before Motoko's departure, Joyce took her for a now familiar walk around the block. Walking arm in arm, Motoko said in her broken English, "Joyce, there is so much on my heart I want to say, . . . but I don't know how to say it. I will always remember The Lighthouse. Thank you for telling me about Jesus. When Motoko go to Japan, I want to find husband just like Morgan!"

Joyce's prayer for a ministry to Orientals was truly answered by God—and in an abundant manner. Instead of just one blessing, He had sent four!

CHAPTER

23

Lice, Scabies, Worms and TB

ONE FALL DAY IN 1982, the doorbell at The Lighthouse rang. Opening the door, Joyce was surprised to see a nursing friend. "Excuse me for bothering you, Joyce," the woman began, looking embarrassed, "but I had to come see you."

"Why don't you come in and have a cup of coffee?" Joyce said.

Settling down in a chair, Joyce's friend began, "As you know, I sponsored a Vietnamese family to come to America. They are arriving soon from a refugee camp in the Philippines. I had made arrangements for them to stay in a small cottage on my father's farm, but he passed away just a short time ago. Now, to settle the estate, we have to sell his land and the house. The Vietnamese family won't have anywhere to live. If I don't find a new sponsor for this family, they will have to return to the Philippines. They have suffered so much that I hate to see them returned. I have been praying about the situation for three straight nights, and every time I prayed, your face came to my mind. I'm not asking you to take the family, but with your connections, maybe you know someone who would."

123

"Well," Joyce said, "I don't know of anyone who could take them in, but let me ask Morgan when he comes home. I will call you if anyone comes to mind." As she said this, something in Joyce's head clicked. *Is this something God might want us to be involved in?*

After the woman left, Joyce prayed, "Lord, if it is Your will for this Vietnamese family to live with us, have Morgan be as touched as I am. That will be the sign for me to know Your will."

That afternoon, Joyce anxiously looked out the window. She could hardly wait for Morgan to pull into the driveway. When he finally arrived, Joyce rushed to meet him before he could get out of his truck. "I have something to tell you," she began. Then she proceeded to tell Morgan, still sitting in the driver's seat, the story of the Vietnamese family.

"When will they be coming?" Morgan asked.

"I guess they are already on their way," Joyce replied. "But, Morgan, financially we are at rock bottom right now. Can we afford to support an entire family?"

"That's the Lord's problem!" Morgan said. "He brought this family to our attention, and somehow He will supply."

So the decision was made, and soon the Vietnamese family arrived in America and moved into The Lighthouse. The family consisted of Tam, the father; Lien, the mother; Tich, the grandmother; Tri, the oldest son; and Tin, the youngest son. A big black garbage bag contained the total of their possessions. The only one who could speak any English at all was Tam. When they arrived and he saw The Lighthouse, he blurted out, "A mansion!"

That same day, Joyce received a phone call offering her a job as a private-duty nurse for a month. When she hung up the phone, she praised God. The Lord had already started supplying their needs! That month of work would pay for all the expenses needed for the Vietnamese family.

The nursing job was to start in two days, and Joyce knew she had much work to do. She called up the public school to arrange enrollment for the two boys. Then she rushed the family to the store to buy the children some school clothes.

Returning home, Joyce gave the entire family a crash course in American life. She taught them how to use appliances such as the mixer, microwave, stove, washer and dryer. She also showed Lien where the cereal, milk and bowls were stored, so she could serve her family breakfast the next morning. Shopping for food would be done the next day.

The first cultural shock for the Ilgenfritz family came at 5:30 the next morning, when they awakened to what sounded like a drill team. The entire Vietnamese family had assembled for their morning calisthenics—a regimen started in the Philippine refugee camp. At six o'clock, Joyce entered the kitchen to find them seated around the table. In the middle of the table was a plate piled high with Cheerios. Each family member was eating the cereal a piece at time, grimacing as if in pain with each bite. When she asked them why they did not use milk, she learned that they did not like it.

"What do you like for breakfast?" Joyce asked.

"Well," Tam began, "in Vietnam, we eat cabbage cooked with garlic and noodles. Could we fix here?"

"Okay," Joyce said, surprised. "When we go to the grocery store this afternoon, we can purchase those items."

The next morning the second shock came—the pungent smell of garlic and cabbage cooking!

During the first several days at The Lighthouse, Tam tried to tell Joyce his family's story, but failed to communicate effectively because of his poor command of the English language. Spotting a typewriter, he sat down and typed out his story in broken English and gave it to Joyce to read.

Tam's family had waited for three months to be smuggled out of Saigon. Then on June 24, 1981, their opportunity came. They were loaded onto a small boat with 62 other people, paying their fare to the captain in gold. While at sea, the boat was intercepted by the military police. Boarding the boat, they threatened to force it to return to Vietnam. Being forewarned of their tactics, one of the men offered the officers gold, which they readily agreed to accept. When two ounces were produced, the head officer laughed and spat in the man's face. Two more ounces were added to the pot, and again the officer laughed, this time spitting in the ocean. After this a heavy packet of gold was produced, and the police, now satisfied, allowed them to leave.

Three days later, the boat still had not reached its destination, and the people grew restless, fearing that they were lost. Their meager rations had dwindled to nearly nothing, and Tam began rationing water to his family.

On the fourth day, they encountered a storm that raged for five hours. No one was injured, but the boat was badly damaged and spirits were low.

When the seas calmed, they spotted a boat in the distance. They signaled for help, but when it drew alongside, the boat people were shocked to find it was piloted by Thai pirates. The pirates boarded the boat and began searching for valuables. After uncovering these, the pirates then proceeded to rape a number of the younger women and teenage girls. One young girl was even killed. Lien had been spared only because she had covered herself with soup and fish sauce and dressed in men's clothing.

Finally the pirates left, and the boat continued its haphazard journey toward freedom. The next day, they spotted another boat. With the memory of the previous day's experience still fresh in their minds, they did not signal for help. The other boat saw them, though, and raced after them. Soon it had caught up, and the Vietnamese boat was once again boarded by pirates. Because the others pirates had taken everything of value, this group could find nothing to take but the boat motor. When the people pleaded with them, however, they returned the motor and left.

After seven days and nights at sea, an oil tanker finally rescued them near Malaysia. The ship took them to Malaysia, where they spent six months in a refugee camp. At that point, another camp in the Philippines accepted them, and from there they came to the United States.

As she finished reading the testimony, Joyce could not believe all that the family had been through. She now felt assured that the Lord had indeed led them to The Lighthouse.

The family seemed to adjust quickly to American life, and things settled into something of a routine. Their stay proved to be both an entertaining and educational experience for the Ilgenfritzes. Tam and his family made an extreme effort to be cordial and helpful. One day Tam approached Joyce saying, "You go work. We stay home and take care of mansion!"

"OK," Joyce answered, hesitantly. "Today, you can clean your bathroom."

Tam misunderstood her in his translation, thinking she had requested that they clean her bedroom. So the family went to work. The sloppiest area was the desk. Joyce had begun sorting bills and other important papers into different piles. To Tam, the papered desk looked like a refuse pile, and he proceeded to "clean it up." When Joyce returned home, she saw that her bedroom had been cleaned. With horror, she noticed her desktop was empty. *Where are the papers I was sorting?* she asked herself. Then Tam and the conversation that morning popped into her head. Knocking on their bedroom door, Joyce asked, "Tam, did you clean my room?"

"Yes!" he replied cheerfully.

"Where are the papers that were on my desk?" Joyce asked.

"Oh, in garbage," he responded. "They were old papers with '81 on them. It is '82! You don't need old papers."

"Oh yes I do!" Joyce said, trying to maintain her composure. "Go get them!"

Tam went out to the curb, retrieved the garbage bag and brought it into the kitchen. He poured its contents onto the kitchen floor and started sorting through it. Eventually, he recovered all of the "old" papers.

One day Joyce and Lien were sitting in the kitchen trying to talk to each other. Suddenly Lien noticed Joyce's wedding ring. She asked Joyce to remove it and then rushed out of the room.

"Lien, where are you going?" Joyce asked in a panicked voice.

"I be right back!" she exclaimed.

Lien went to the bathroom, picked up her toothbrush and proceeded to polish Joyce's ring. When she returned, she presented Joyce with her now shiny ring.

Tich, the grandmother, wanted to help out, too. To keep her busy, Tam would assign her the sidewalks and driveway to sweep. When Joyce came home from work, Tich would run up to her and announce, "I comb your driveway!"

One day Tich came into the kitchen smiling. She grabbed a light-colored dish towel, wet it under the faucet and headed out the door. In a few minutes, she returned. The towel was now nearly black with dirt. Washing it under the faucet again, she hurried back out the door. After four of these trips, Joyce's curiosity overcame her, and she watched Tich out a window. There, in the driveway, Tich was washing Joyce's car, wipe by wipe with the same dish towel. When it became dirty, she would return to the house and rinse it off. After completing her task, she rinsed the towel a final time, hung it in its original spot, smiled warmly and left. Joyce could not help but laugh as she placed the towel in the dirty clothes hamper.

Events surrounding the Vietnamese family's stay were not always so humorous, though. No one laughed the day the school nurse informed Joyce that Tri and Tin had lice! That night Joyce examined all 14 residents of The Lighthouse. She found lice in Morgan's and Dwayne's beards as well as in everyone else's hair. It was a unique affair, shampooing each head with a special shampoo, then carefully combing each other's hair with a fine tooth comb. Just when they thought the problem was solved, another outbreak occurred, resulting in yet another shampooing and combing.

This second shampooing exhausted Joyce. Just before she was ready to do her hair, she discovered the shampoo bottle was empty. Frustrated, she decided to go to the drugstore for a new bottle and hurried to the car. Backing around the curve in their driveway, Joyce scraped her hubcaps against the driveway's stone wall. The loud crunch caused Morgan to look up from his yardwork and yell, "Don't you ever use your rearview mirrors?"

That was all Joyce needed to hear, and she broke down in tears. She got out of the car and went back into the house. Hearing the commotion, Tam came to check on Joyce. "We sorry we give you lice," Tam apologized.

"It's OK, Tam. That's not why I am crying,"

Joyce assured them as she retreated to her bedroom. A few minutes later, there was a knock on the bedroom door. When Joyce opened it, she found all five members of the Vietnamese family standing there.

"We sorry we give you lice!" they said in unison.

"I am not crying about that," Joyce replied with tears running down her cheeks.

"Why you cry?" Tam asked.

"Because my husband is angry with me!"

"Oh!" they all said. Then Lien rushed out the front door, grabbed Morgan and dragged him to the bedroom. She pushed him next to Joyce and made a motion for them to kiss. As they kissed, all of Tam's family stood by smiling!

A week after the lice epidemic, Lien complained about her finger itching. Upon examining her hands, Joyce diagnosed scabies. Not only did they have to shampoo and wash everyone again with another special solution, but everything in the house had to be scrubbed with—or washed in—a disinfect: drapes, chairs, rugs, matresses, clothing, sheets, towels—everything!

That night, near exhaustion and with only one more blanket to disinfect, Joyce collapsed into a chair. "Why don't we just put this blanket into a garbage bag, set it outside and finish it tomorrow," Morgan suggested. "You need to get some rest."

After this was done, they went to bed. That night it was cold, and Tam thought his family needed another blanket. Not wanting to disturb Joyce, he went outside, brought inside the infected blanket, and covered his family. The next morning, when Joyce found what Tam had done, she was furious. What could she do, though, but take it in stride? She then proceeded to reshampoo, rewash and redisinfect everybody and thing in the house.

Just when things were settling back to normal, the Vietnamese family found out they had worms. Then, Tich received a tuberculosis test, and the results came back positive. Every time someone coughed, Joyce imagined that the person had TB. She became concerned one day when she noticed Morgan's frequent coughing. Her fears increased when he started sweating heavily at night. Both were signs of TB. Then they discovered what the real problem was—the controls on the electric blanket had gotten switched, and Joyce kept turning up her thermostat because she was cold!

After laughing over the discovery, Morgan turned to Joyce and exclaimed, "You know, living here at The Lighthouse is exciting. I never know what to expect. First it was lice, then scabies and worms and now TB!"

Tam announced to Joyce one day that he had established five goals for himself and his family upon arrival in the United States. First, he wanted everyone to learn English. Second, he wanted his children to attend school and do well. Third, he desired a job—he refused to consider welfare, even taking offense when Joyce mentioned it. Fourth, he hoped one day to have his own home. And last, he wanted a car. He planned to become totally independent, thereby showing his sincere appreciation to the Ilgenfritzes and to the American government for allowing him to come to the United States.

One by one, the Lord answered his prayers for these needs. In a short time, he was being tutored in English through the Literacy Council. Several mothers from the elementary school volunteered time to tutor Tri and Tin, and soon, the children were well established in school.

Tam's occupation in Vietnam was as a pharmacist, and Joyce inquired at the York Hospital about a possible job opening. There was one, and Tam had his first American job.

A car was donated to them by a member of The Christian and Missionary Alliance Church of York. After several weeks, they were able to rent a home in the same school district. The Lord even provided furniture and appliances through the Ilgenfritzes' friends and members of their church. When this last need was met, Tam showed his thankfulness to God by literally falling on his knees and praising Him.

In spite of all their trials, these two families from different cultures had learned to live together in harmony because of Christ's love. That Christmas they gathered in Tam's home for a time of celebration and praise. They trimmed the Christmas tree together and shared gifts with each other. The Ilgenfritzes' gift for Tam's family was a nativity scene. As they placed the figure of Baby Jesus in the center, Joyce thought of how He had been the center of both families' lives. He had miraculously provided for their needs and brought them through both the bad times and the good times.

24

The 38-year-old Secret

THE LAST JAPANESE GIRL who came to live at The Lighthouse was Tomie (Toe me a). She came to America in the fall of 1982, to attend York College. On registration day at the college, Joyce secured permission from the administrators to set up a table for international students. Those who stopped by her table were invited to a picnic at The Lighthouse. Twenty-five students came, and one of them was Tomie.

Joyce could tell that Tomie was overwhelmed by the new experience of college life in a foreign country, so she tried to talk with Tomie and make her feel at ease. Before Tomie left, Joyce told her that she wanted to be her American mother.

Tomie visited The Lighthouse occasionally, and over the Christmas holidays, she stayed with the Ilgenfritzes. During that time, Joyce had a number of chances to speak with her about the Lord, and on December 31, Tomie accepted Christ as her Savior. After that, she attended church regularly with them.

On the last Sunday before her return to Japan, the pastor called her forward and had a special prayer for her. That evening, a film about Eric

Little—the main character in the movie *Chariots of Fire*—was shown in the church. The film told about his death in a Japanese concentration camp and showed scenes of the Japanese attack on Pearl Harbor. It was not a particularly uplifting evening for Tomie. To make matters worse, that morning one of the men of the church, a Mr. Kline, had approached Joyce and asked her and Morgan if they would bring Tomie to his house that night after church. He said he had a gift he wanted Tomie to take back to Japan with her. Joyce could tell that Tomie was nervous about the mysterious request.

During the drive to Mr. Kline's house, Tomie silently stared out the car window. Sensing that something was wrong, Morgan asked if she was OK.

"No," she replied, "I am bothered by that film we saw tonight. It did not show the Japanese people in a very good light."

"Don't let it bother you," Morgan assured her. "The boys in the Japanese army were only doing what their country asked them to do. Just like Americans, they were loyal citizens fighting for their country."

Somewhat reassured, Tomie asked Joyce, "What do think Mr. Kline wants?"

"I don't know," Joyce replied, "it sounds kind of strange, doesn't it?"

Soon they arrived at the Klines', and Morgan turned into the driveway. At the front door, they were greeted by Mr. Kline and his wife and invited in. After cordial greetings and trivial conversation, Mr. Kline suddenly became serious. He brought out a box and a letter. Handing the letter to Joyce, he asked, "Joyce, would you please read this letter? It is the fifth draft I have written to Tomie, but I still don't think it says what I want to tell her. I don't think I could read it without becoming emotional."

"Sure," Joyce said as she opened the envelope. Taking out the letter, she began to read:

June 19, 1983

Dear Tomie:

When I learned that you plan to return to your homeland soon, a small clear voice told me to write this to you.

I was born and raised on a 100-acre farm here in York County. I was the next to the youngest of eight children. My parents taught us to respect the Lord's Day and to go to church.

I used to love listening to our battery-operated radio, and one of my favorites programs featured the singing group, "The Morlan Sisters." One Sunday afternoon—December 7, 1941, to be exact—my father and I were listening to this program when the announcer broke in and told us that the Japanese had just bombed Pearl Harbor.

I quickly asked Dad, "Where is Pearl Harbor?" He hesitated, as we looked at each other. Then I knew he did not know. We both, however, knew it was not good. Dad did not say anything else and soon left to feed the stock. The following day, I found out where Pearl Harbor was located. Even though it was thousands of miles away, it almost seemed like they had bombed our farm.

I suddenly wondered how God could allow such a thing to happen and on a Sunday at that! Then I surmised that this terrible thing must be of Satan—not God. We had been taught in Sunday school that God stands for good things and that Satan represented the bad things. This event was not good, so it had to come from Satan.

After this, I became very bitter. Hate was the order of the day. I began to secretly hate the Japanese people.

The war escalated, and as my friends and relatives answered the call to defend our country, my bitterness and hate increased. My one brother, Allen, was already in the Army, and my brother Bill was about to leave for training. Somehow, I had to get more involved in getting even with the Japanese. But how? I had just turned 16 and was still not old enough to enlist.

One day I made up my mind to try to enlist, and I hitched a ride to the York recruiting office. They quickly turned down my application and sent me home, but I learned what I had to do to enlist before my 17th birthday. I obtained the necessary documents and hitched a ride to another recruiting station in Lancaster. I was finally accepted into the Navy. I was on my way to satisfying my bitterness and hate.

After months of schooling and training, I was assigned to the Navy amphibian fleet, and when I learned we were sailing to the South Pacific, I was excited and delighted. Our job was to shell beaches at night, then land troops and supplies as soon as daylight arrived.

As my buddies were injured or killed, my hate

increased. Even the 12 Japanese planes that we shot down did not satisfy me. I wanted to kill as many Japanese as I could. After the atomic bomb was dropped, I thrilled over the number of casualties. What difference did it make if innocent women and children were killed? They were Japanese, and they had it coming.

I was part of the occupying force, and after arriving in Japan, we set out to cause further destruction. Even after the peace treaty was signed, we still continued, burning office buildings, destroying civilian equipment, wrecking homes.

Though we had won the war, I was still not satisfied. During those years in the South Pacific, I looked upon the Japanese people as something less than human. I could not see beyond my hate to realize that they were people like me. They had obeyed their leaders just like we had. They suffered just like we suffered.

It has taken me the last 38 years to learn these things. And now, I want you to know that I love you and your people. I ask that you and your people forgive me for my hate and bitterness. I have forgiven your people for their actions. Accepting Jesus Christ as my Savior made that forgiveness possible.

Tomie, when you go back to Japan, you will be teaching and will come in contact with many people. You will have many opportunities to witness for Jesus. Tell them of Jesus' love and of my love for them.

I am sorry that I have not had the chance to know you better during your stay in our country. We thank God for Joyce and Morgan Ilgen-

fritz. How you crossed paths, I do not know. But I do know that the Lord was in it. Otherwise, I would not have had this opportunity to talk to you and your people.

Finally Tomie, my wife and I want you to have these three flags. First, is the Christian flag.

Joyce paused from reading while Tomie opened the lid to the box and pulled out a Christian flag. She held it up and looked at it, then draped it over her lap as Joyce continued to read.

Somehow, if you and I can be instrumental in keeping the Christian flag above all other banners, then we know that Christ is truly the Head of our countries.

The second flag is a Japanese flag.

Again, Joyce stopped reading as Tomie carefully lifted the flag out of the box, unfolding it, displaying the huge red sun centered in a field of white. Then Joyce resumed her reading.

I return it to you for your disposition. I collected a number of these flags from dead Japanese soldiers. This is the only one I have left. Many Japanese soldiers had such a flag wrapped around their bodies under their uniforms. I understand that the names written on the flags were members of their families or friends.

Tomie's eyes swelled with tears as she read what was written on the flag—the well wishes of this soldier's family and friends. When she discovered a bullet hole and saw the dried blood around it, she wept openly. After a few moments, she reached down into the box and pulled out the last flag. Joyce continued to read.

The last flag is our American flag. With it, I hope you remember your time here in the States. May all of these flags be symbolic of our love to you and your people, and above all, symbolic of the great unparalleled love that Jesus Christ has shown for all people around the world. God bless you as you go!

With tears still in her eyes, Tomie looked at Mr. Kline, held up the Japanese flag and said, "Sir, I have never seen a flag like this one except in a museum. I do not know what to do with it, but there is one thing I promise you. When I return to Japan, I will search diligently for this soldier's family. If necessary, I will have it announced on radio and television and printed in the newspaper until they are found. Then I will give them these flags as a symbol of what Jesus has done for you by taking away your hate for the Japanese people."

That week Tomie left for a sightseeing tour of the United States, then she returned to Japan. Joyce received several letters from her during the summer, but Tomie's efforts to find the soldier's family proved fruitless.

Then one day Joyce went to the mailbox and discovered a thick envelope from Japan. Inside were two newspaper clippings sent by Tomie. Being in Japanese, Tomie had translated the message—the soldier's widow had been found! The headline of the first clipping, dated August 14, 1983, read: "The Japanese flag which was taken by American soldiers brought back by

Japanese girl who studied in the States—Will Japanese forgive? ex-soldier asks."

The second article, dated September 20, 1983, stated: "The flag which belongs to the spirit of the war dead, finally returns to the wife's arms after 40 years." The article also included a photograph of the soldier and his widow.

Tomie's accompanying letter filled in the details. The soldier, Ogino Shinyu, and his wife were married in 1940 while he was a cook in a department store in Kyoto. He moved to Nagoya where he worked in the kitchen of a military factory, while his wife stayed in Kyoto. While there, he received his draft notice, so he returned to Kyoto to stay with his wife and family for a week before leaving for training camp. In August 1943, at the age of 31, he was sent to China. A year later, he requested assignment as close as possible to Japan. His request was granted, and he went to Okinawa. Records at the Chumichi Newspaper and the Ministry of Welfare showed that he had died there on August 13, 1945, three days before the end of World War 2.

It was not until the end of 1945 that his wife received his last letter and not until 1949, that she received official notification of his death.

And so the gospel of reconciliation that changed a broken, repentant World War 2 veteran was conveyed through a young Japanese Christian girl to a Japanese soldier's widow and to the Japanese nation.

25

Our "Little Orphan Annie"

NOT EVERY LIGHTHOUSE guest had a happy ending to his or her story. One such individual first came to The Lighthouse as a little girl. Because her story paralleled that of the comic strip character, she came to be known at The Lighthouse as Annie.

Annie's mother, whom we will call Lucille, had come to The Lighthouse in 1978—one of the pregnant young women from New Life for Girls. Joyce and Morgan had attended a New Life Christian party and had noticed Lucille walking around looking sad. After meeting and talking with her, Morgan decided that they should ask her to live at The Lighthouse. Impressed at first by her sincerity, Joyce soon sensed that Lucille's commitment to Christ was shallow and that she had some serious spiritual problems. Lucille had her baby—her fourth—then returned to New Life for Girls.

Several months later, in 1979, Lucille contacted The Ilgenfritzes and asked if she could come to live at The Lighthouse again. She and her baby—and two other daughters, one eight and the other seven (the fourth daughter lived with her grandmother)—had no place to live and needed a home.

Joyce and Morgan finally decided to let her come. Joyce believed the Lord brought her back because of the children.

The family room in the basement became a little apartment for the new arrivals. Joyce sat down with Lucille, and together they went over the rules of the house and wrote out a list of goals that would enable her to become a good mother. Joyce agreed to help her with the older children while they worked on her role as a mother.

After only a week, though, the covenant fell through. Soon, Joyce found herself doing all the work in caring for the children, while Lucille slept late. Joyce helped the two older children get dressed for school and packed their lunches. She also cared for the baby during the morning hours.

Lucille and her children stayed at The Lighthouse for a year, and during that time things fell into sort of a routine. Joyce continued to share the bulk of the children's care because she was concerned for them. One of the girls—the seven-year-old, whom they nicknamed Annie—became especially close to the Ilgenfritz family. Eventually, Lucille found a furnished apartment and moved from The Lighthouse. It began to look like another happy ending as she became more and more independent.

Then word reached Joyce that Lucille had returned to her old life on the streets. During this time, Joyce tried to keep in contact with the older children, but Lucille moved and even this contact was lost.

One day about a year later, Joyce received a phone call from Lucille. Because Lucille knew that the Ilgenfritzes had had a special love for her seven-year-old, she asked if they would raise the girl. Joyce told Lucille that she would talk to Morgan and call her back the next day. After prayer that night, they decided to take the girl in.

The next day, Joyce and Morgan went to pick up little Annie. They prepared a special room for her, went out and bought new clothes and reenrolled her in York Christian School. Then Joyce notified the welfare office of Annie's new home.

When Lucille discovered a reduction in the monthly support checks, she exploded in rage. She immediately phoned the Ilgenfritzes and demanded that the child be returned. Annie cried when Joyce told her that her mother wanted her back, but there was nothing they could do.

Several of the Oriental girls were living at The Lighthouse at this time, and they became upset over Annie's leaving. They had all taken an interest in her, sewing clothing for her, getting her room ready and fixing her hair. The day Annie went for a haircut, they all went along to watch. Annie had never had this much attention before, and she loved it.

The day before Annie's departure, Hing, the Chinese student who lived across the street, asked Joyce, "Do you think if I prayed to God for this girl, He would hear me?"

"Yes," Joyce assured her, "God will hear your prayers!"

When Hing saw Annie's mother pull in the driveway the next day, she immediately warned

Joyce over the phone, pleading for Joyce to hide the girl. As Morgan talked to Lucille, Joyce asked the girls to go upstairs to help Annie finish packing.

While packing, the girls tried to figure out ways Annie could get in contact with the Ilgenfritzes if she needed help. They came up with the idea of placing The Lighthouse's phone number in Annie's shoe. After Annie left, a gloomy depression settled over the house.

Six months later, the phone rang. Joyce picked it up and was surprised by Annie's voice. "Joyce," she said, "I am in a phone booth. I still have your phone number in my shoe. Mommy is in jail. I am with Grandma. She says her nerves are bad and that I must find some place to go. Could I come for a weekend?"

"Yes, of course!" Joyce exclaimed excitedly.

When Annie arrived, she told Joyce and Morgan of the horrible living conditions at her grandmother's house. By now, her mother had had two other children—all were girls—and the six girls, the grandmother and two Cuban refugees lived in a small apartment. All of Annie's sisters were dark skinned, but she had a light complexion. Because of this, they had cruelly nicknamed her "Honky." There was also neither heat nor lights because the electric bill had not been paid in months. Candlelight served as their only source of light and heat.

Joyce tried to become friends with Annie's grandmother, offering to take her to the doctor and other places of necessity. After she saw that Joyce really cared about her—and about Annie—she allowed Annie to stay at The Lighthouse for several days at a time. Finally, she consented for Annie to live at The Lighthouse full-time.

Everyone at The Lighthouse rejoiced. During this stay, Annie's birthday month came up, and as the big day approached, excitment filled the air. Birthday presents were purchased, wrapped and placed in her room with the understanding that she would not open them until the day arrived.

Then, just before her birthday, Annie's mother appeared, demanding Annie and her clothes. Lucille had been released from jail, and she and her mother had decided to move to Chicago.

Packing this time seemed unbearable, especially with the unopened birthday gifts sitting on the dresser. Joyce told Annie, "I know it's not the Lord's timing yet, but someday, we will have you back. You have our telephone number memorized, so call us collect if you need something, honey. Here are some stamped, addressed envelopes with writing paper. Make sure you write to us."

As Annie prepared to leave, no one could keep from crying, and it was all Joyce could do to keep from running after her as she got into the car. Joyce's only comfort was knowing that three weeks earlier, Annie had accepted Jesus as her personal Savior. Amy, Beth and Joyce had all prayed with her.

A week later, Joyce took Amy and Beth to see the film *Annie*. Driving home with tear-filled eyes, they could not help but think about their own little Annie.

Nearly a whole year passed without any word. Annie had not written or called, but Joyce refused to quit praying for her. She still believed that someday Annie would return.

Then one day the phone rang. The operator said there was a collect call from California. Puzzled, Joyce accepted the call. When she heard Annie's voice, she broke into tears. "Annie!" Joyce sobbed, "Where are you?"

"I'm in California. We came here a few months ago. My mother is in jail again. Could I come and stay with you for the summer? My grandma said it would be OK."

"Sure you can come," Joyce replied. "I'll make the arrangements, then call you back."

Joyce purchased an airline ticket, arranging for Annie to pick it up at the airport in California. Once again, there was great rejoicing when Annie was reunited with The Lighthouse family. Her clothes went back into the familiar dresser, and soon, she was back in the routine of life at The Lighthouse and accepted as a family member. During her absence, though, Annie had changed. She was no longer the innocent little girl they had first known, but a budding teenager.

As the summer progressed, calls back to California revealed that her grandmother was going to let her stay at The Lighthouse—permanently! Again, Joyce enrolled her in York Christian school, and they went shopping for clothes.

Just before school started, however, bad news came. A court order arrived summoning Annie back to California. She had to be a witness in her mother's upcoming trial. Spirits slumped. Joyce and Morgan contacted a lawyer, who tried to block the California court's demand, saying that she could give a written or recorded testimony. At first the court agreed, but about the time her staying seemed secure, a notice arrived—Annie must return to California.

Though the situation was not as bad as the times before when Annie's mother forced her to leave, there were ample tears as she boarded her plane. As Annie waved goodbye to Joyce and Morgan, they held on to the hope that she might soon return to live with them.

26

Joyce Learns a New Lesson

AUGUST 1984, WAS A warm month. In the back of a small restaurant, Joyce and Morgan were enjoying an elegant dinner. The special occasion was in honor of their 26th wedding anniversary. Reminiscing over the past years, they recalled how hot it had been on their wedding day—104 degrees! They talked about each of their four children and the many people who had lived with them at The Lighthouse.

They also remembered the day nine years ago, when they told the Lord, "We will do anything You want us to do." The years since that the time, they decided, had been much better than those prior to it. Jesus' presence made the difference.

After a relaxed dinner, they summoned the waiter, paid their bill and got up to leave. As Morgan helped Joyce with the chair, Joyce noticed a stiff, numb feeling in her legs. She managed to stand up and walk to the car, but with some difficulty. When she got there, she felt nearly drained. She did not tell Morgan for fear it would spoil this special evening. After a while, Joyce dismissed the feeling, deciding that sitting in the restaurant for nearly four hours had caused the problem.

Two days later, though, the stiffness and numb feeling returned, this time accompanied by double vision, dizziness, a terrible headache, extreme muscle weakness and very little physical coordination. Morgan phoned the doctor who had her immediately admitted to the York Hospital.

In an effort to diagnose her illness, the doctors conducted test after test. Joyce, with her background in nursing, feared a brain tumor. Finally, after nearly a week in the hospital, the neurologist and his assistant entered her room.

"I have your diagnosis," the doctor said hesitantly. "You have multiple sclerosis."

"Oh," Joyce commented, her voice catching in her throat. "Well . . . I can live with that!"

"You can live with that?" the doctor repeated questioningly. "I don't think you know what you are saying."

"I am just thankful that it's not a brain tumor," Joyce responded.

"Yes," he agreed, "but just wait until a few months go by and the full impact hits you. This is a very serious condition."

"I know it is; I was trained as a nurse," Joyce replied. "I know how serious it is."

"I just don't think you realize," he insisted, turning to his assistant. "Look at her. I told her she has M.S., and she says she is going to live with it. These M.S. patients! They want to be so strong." With that, he turned to leave.

"Look Doctor," Joyce blurted out, "I want to tell you something. I am not a strong person. I am a very weak person. I want you to know that. But I also want you to know that I have a very strong God, and He's going to help me!"

After the doctor's departure, Joyce gave a sigh of relief. She was somehow comforted to know that she did not have a brain tumor. Now, though, she was confronted with the problem of multiple sclerosis. Being a nurse really only made matters worse. She began to remember all the M.S. patients she had cared for during her nursing work. Her aunt had contracted the disease at age 40. She had lived 20 more years, but they had not been pleasant.

Suddenly these thoughts overwhelmed Joyce, and she broke down. Trying to combat these feelings, she told herself, *God's Word has to be my comfort, my strength and my shield. I have to now stand on all these spiritual truths I know intellectually. I know who God is, and He is going to help me through this situation.*

Joyce picked up her Bible and turned to John 15.

> I am the true vine and my Father is the gardener. He cuts off every branch in me that bears no fruit, while every branch that does bear fruit he trims clean so that it will be even more fruitful. No branch can bear fruit by itself; it must remain in the vine. (John 15:1–2; 4)

Jesus is the vine, Joyce thought to herself, *and I am a branch. I can do nothing apart from Him.* Slowly a peace and an assurance came over her. No longer could she think about tomorrow, the next week or even when she would return home. She could only think about today. *If God is who He said He is, He will help me through today. He*

*is in control. Even if I am not healed, He will give
me the strength to carry on.*

Aware that some drastic changes were about to
take place in her life, Joyce began to prepare herself mentally. Because of her double vision, she
was unable to read. She was not going to give up
the Bible, though. She sent Morgan to buy Bible
tapes and then had him bring her tape recorder
to the hospital.

One afternoon she was listening to the tape of
Psalm 119. Verse 11 was one of her favorites: "I
have hidden your word in my heart that I might
not sin against you." As she heard these words, it
suddenly became clear that worrying was a sin,
and it could cause a break in her fellowship with
God. She realized that it was like telling God that
she did not think He was big enough to handle
this. "Lord," Joyce prayed, "Your Word is in my
heart! Help me not to sin against You."

Psalm 139 became Joyce's most comforting
passage:

> O Lord, you have searched me
>   and you know me.
> You know when I sit and when I rise;
>   you perceive my thoughts from afar.
> You discern my going out and my lying down;
>   you are familiar with all my ways.
> Before a word is on my tongue
>   you know it completely, O Lord.
>
> You hem me in, behind and before;
>   you have laid your hand upon me.
> Such knowledge is too wonderful for me,
>   too lofty for me to attain.

Where can I go from your Spirit?
  Where can I flee from your presence?
If I go up to the heavens, you are there;
  if I make my bed in the depths, you are
  there.
If I rise on the wings of the dawn,
  if I settle on the far side of the sea,
even there your hand will guide me,
  your right hand will hold me fast.

If I say, "Surely the darkness will hide me
  and the light become night around me,"
even the darkness will not be dark to you;
  the night will shine like day,
  for darkness is as light to you.

For you created my inmost being;
  you knit me together in my mother's
  womb.
I praise you because I am fearfully and won-
derfully made;
  your works are wonderful,
  I know that full well.
My frame was not hidden from you
  when I was made in the secret place.
When I was woven together in the depths of
the earth,
  your eyes saw my unformed body.
All the days ordained for me
  were written in your book
  before one of them came to be.

After reading the Psalm, Joyce would pray,
"Jesus, I know that You have a perfect plan for my
life. How can multiple sclerosis fit into this plan? I
want to know."

Because of Joyce's nursing experience, she had, at one time or another, worked in nearly every department in the hospital, and she knew many of the staff members. Only three nights before she first became ill, she had worked private duty at the hospital. Ironically, she now occupied the room that was just a few doors down the hall from the room in which she earlier worked.

Word quickly spread throughout the hospital of Joyce's illness. Even though a "No Visitors" sign hung on her door, the hospital staff ignored it, and Joyce seemed to have a constant stream of nurses visiting her. After her diagnosis, several of her closer nurse friends came to her room. "Joyce," one said, with tears in her eyes, "we cannot believe this has happened to you."

Another one became especially upset. "Look at all you have done for the Lord. Now, when you need Him the most, where is He?" she protested. "I am really angry at God."

"Don't be upset," Joyce replied quickly. "Those things weren't done in vain, and I didn't do them so God would do something for me. I did them because that's what He asked of me. I don't have the right to question God as to why this happened. I can only believe that it is His will for my life."

One afternoon, Joyce told her doctor, "The 'No Visitors' sign must go."

"But Joyce," he protested, "if I take that sign off of your door, the whole county will come and see you! The strain will not be good for you."

"I don't care about that," Joyce pleaded. "People are paying to park, and they come up to the room only to find they can't come in. I don't think that is fair. These are people who care about me and whom I care for. They should at least be able to stick their heads in the door."

The doctor thought for a moment, then said, "I'll tell you what, Joyce. Instead of the 'No Visitors' sign, I'll have the nurses hang up a '5 Minute Visits Only' sign. But you'll have to promise me that the visitors will follow that rule."

"OK," Joyce agreed.

As the different individuals came to call on her—many of whom Joyce had not seen for several years—she began to see God's hand in it. One day she prayed, "Lord, now I am beginning to see that all of this was part of Your plan. There was no other way I could have seen and talked to all of my old friends. Thank You, Father."

Even the Vietnamese family came to visit. The boys, dressed up in their Sunday suits, gave Joyce a crocheted pillow with the word "Love" inscribed on it.

On one Sunday, 30 different people came to visit. Before they left, each one took Joyce's hand and prayed with her. By the end of the day, she was exhausted, but she told Morgan, "Having all of these visitors is tiring, but I sincerely appreciate their prayers. I know the power of prayer."

When it looked as if Joyce would be allowed to go home soon, her family doctor came in to speak with her. He was a Christian and made regular visits to Joyce's room.

"Joyce," he began, "you know you will have to give up your ministry at The Lighthouse. You cannot handle the responsibilities now. Those days are gone."

When she heard these words, Joyce wanted to

cry. Just at that moment, though, her pastor came through the door. Joyce was too upset to talk to anyone else, so she pulled the sheets over her head. Shocked, he asked, "Is there a problem, Joyce?"

The doctor proceeded to tell the pastor what he had told Joyce. Slowly, she lowered the sheets from her face. "Doctor, that is not my ministry, but God's. If He wants me to serve in that ministry, He will have to make me well. I don't think you have the right to say that I have to give it up!"

After the two left the room, the tears Joyce had been holding back rushed out. "Lord," she cried, "I just don't feel that closing The Lighthouse is what You want us to do. I need a sign from You to know that what we are doing is right for us now."

A few minutes later, the bedside phone rang. "Joyce, do you remember me?" a young feminine voice asked.

"Do I remember you!" Joyce said. "Of course I remember you, Jill. How are you?"

Three years ago, Jill had lived at The Lighthouse while her mother had her leg amputated. A social worker had contacted Joyce about taking her in while the mother recuperated. Jill had fallen and broken her arm and had it in a cast during her stay at The Lighthouse.

"Joyce, did you know that my mother died?"

"No, I didn't," Joyce replied. "Where are you calling from?"

"My sister's house. She and I don't get along very well, though. In fact, she said that if I don't leave by Sunday, her husband is going to leave. I have nowhere to go. Could I come to live with you?"

The timing of that question was perfect. It was the sign Joyce had prayed for. "The doctor told me I shouldn't have any stress," Joyce said, not wanting to build up Jill's hopes, but feeling over-joyed on the inside.

"I won't cause you any problems," Jill promised. "Please let me come."

"I'll have to talk with my husband and my doctor and pray about it," Joyce said. "Call me back tomorrow."

A few minutes later, Beth burst into Joyce's room, "Mother, did someone just call you on the phone?"

"Yes," Joyce replied.

"Well, she called me too! What do you think?"

"I'm not sure," Joyce said. "What do you think?"

"It may sound strange, Mother, but I have never been so sure of something in my life as I am of this. I know the Lord wants Jill to come to live with us. I know I can help her. I am so sick of being the baby of the family. It would be so nice being a big sister. Now it is my turn. I really want Jill to come."

"With my being sick, you know you will have to do most of the work."

"I know it's going to be work," Beth assured her mother, "and I promise to help out."

Morgan walked into the hospital room about this time, arriving for his daily visit. After being briefed on the situation, he concluded, "You know what is going to happen to this girl if we don't take her. She will end up on the streets. We can help that girl. We're not going to give her to the world."

A smile came across Joyce's face. Regardless of what the doctor would say, she knew the sign was complete. In the midst of adversity, the Lord had spoken. Joyce knew now that God was going to heal her. The pieces of the puzzle were fitting together.

The next day, Joyce's roommate had surgery. That afternoon, Joyce volunteered to help feed her. Still having trouble with double vision, Joyce groped her way over to the woman's bed. As she dipped the spoon into the jello and brought it up to the lady's mouth, she hesitated. *Which of the two mouths I see is the right one?* Joyce asked herself. She made a guess but was wrong. Jello soon covered her roommate's face. Finally completing the task, Joyce returned to her bed in defeat.

Lying there, Joyce recalled Hebrews 11—"the Faith Chapter." She remembered verse 1: "Now faith is being sure of what we hope for and certain of what we do not see." She breathed a prayer, asking the Lord to help her have faith.

The next day, when her roommate's husband came to visit, Joyce turned her head away to avoid eye contact. She did not want to have to bother with trying to see someone through her impaired vision. She could not help but overhear their conversation, though. Somehow the man had started talking about Orientals. He was upset over the fact that there were so many foreign cars on the road and felt that Americans should buy American. As he continued to talk, Joyce sensed a deep hatred in his voice. His anger seemed to reach a peak when he exclaimed, "Every little

Japanese car on the road should be blown right off!"

At this remark, Joyce could no longer keep from speaking. Turning over, she asked him, "Excuse me, sir, by chance were you in the battle at Pearl Harbor?"

"Yes, I was!" he boasted.

"I want to thank you for what you did," Joyce said, hoping to gain his confidence. "What you and your compatriots did for our country was outstanding."

"But," Joyce continued, "do you know that you have to forgive the Japanese people? They were only doing what the leaders of their country ordered them to do. They, too, thought themselves to be loyal citizens."

"How can you love the Japanese?" the man asked curiously.

"Because God loves them!"

"I don't believe in God, and I don't believe in Jesus," the man uttered. "I don't believe in any of that!"

"Would you listen if I told you a little story?" Joyce asked.

"Go ahead," the man agreed.

Joyce then told him the story of Tomie and the Japanese flag, explaining how the event had been a healing process for Mr. Kline. The man then admitted of owning several of those same Japanese flags himself.

As Joyce told the story, something miraculous began to happen. Her vision began to clear up! She could actually feel the muscles tightening in her face. Suddenly she felt the presence of the Holy Spirit, and she started witnessing with an unexpected boldness to this man. As he sat and listened, his wife's eyes began to fill with tears.

"Lady," the man said with a quivering voice when Joyce had finished, "I don't pray, but if I ever do, I'll pray for you, because you are a good woman!" With that, he said goodbye to his wife and left.

Joyce's health continued to improve. The day before the doctor was to release her, he came in and told Joyce, "I have to know who will be doing your housework before I let you go home. You must have some help."

"Oh," Joyce said, "a Japanese girl lives with us now, and she will help me with the housework."

As she said these words, Joyce realized how God had provided even before her need. After Tomie had left to go back to Japan, Joyce had prayed that the Lord would send still another Japanese girl. Then, near Christmas, Joyce received a letter from a girl who lived in Tokyo. This girl, named Nabuko, had worked with an American girl who knew the Ilgenfritzes. She asked to come live with the Ilgenfritz family for a year, promising to do their housework in exchange for room and board. Praising God for another answer to prayer, Joyce immediately replied in the affirmative.

Now, as Joyce looked back at the incident, she knew that God's timing was perfect. Nabuko had arrived June 29—a little over a month before Joyce had to go to the hospital. During that time, Joyce taught her how to use the vacuum cleaner, washer, dryer, stove, microwave and other household appliances. She taught her the routine of the house, and soon Nabuko had taken over the housework.

On the day of Joyce's return to The Lighthouse, Amy and Nabuko greeted her at the door with big smiles. "This is the day the Lord has made," Amy pronounced, "we are going to rejoice and be glad!" Arriving home felt so wonderful!

Women from the church brought lunch and supper every day for two weeks, and Joyce treasured the visits with these special friends. She also knew, though, that she had to get back into the routine of cooking the family meals. September was fast approaching, and four college students were due to return to live at The Lighthouse. To prepare herself, Joyce again began to quote Scripture. "I am the Lord who heals you." "Daughter, your faith has healed you." She repeated the Scriptures over and over.

During devotions, she read John 10:10, "The thief comes only to steal and kill and destroy; I have come that they may have life, and have it to the full." Joyce meditated on that Scripture. *The thief,* she thought, *is the devil. He wants to steal my peace of mind, my health, my joy and wants to kill my body and my spirit. I also know that Jesus said that He came that I might have life and have it more abundantly. Jesus is greater than Satan.*

Joyce never once thought that her multiple sclerosis was caused by God. She did, however, know that He had allowed it. She thought of how God had granted Satan permission to do anything to Job except take his life. Even though Satan tried to destroy Job, he never turned against God.

She also recalled the account of Joseph and how he had been betrayed by his brothers and sold into slavery in Egypt. After Jacob died, his sons feared Joseph would take action against them, but Joseph assured them that he held no grudge. "You intended to harm me, but God intended it for good."

God could use the circumstances of multiple sclerosis for good. Joyce believed if God wanted her to function in The Lighthouse, He would give her everything she needed, including strength.

When the four college students moved in, everything went fine for a few days, but then Joyce felt she was losing control of her house. The order she had been careful to establish over the years seemed to be disintegrating. "Lord," she prayed, "I cannot function like this!"

One morning Joyce got out of bed and dressed, despite feeling terrible. "You cannot go on how you feel," she reminded herself. "You have to stand on God's Word." She walked to the kitchen reciting her two verses. She gradually felt better, and as the day progressed, she seemed to grow stronger. Each day after this, she tried to do a little more work, and each day she felt a little stronger.

By the time her monthly checkup came, Joyce was feeling nearly normal. Because of the earlier confrontation, Joyce had made an appointment to see a different neurologist. As the new doctor looked over her records, he asked Joyce how she was feeling.

"Good!" Joyce replied.

As part of his examination, the doctor began to give her a series of standard neurological tests.

About halfway through the tests, he stopped, picked up her chart and examined it with a puzzled look on his face. "Are you sure this is the right chart? It does have your name on it, but nothing on it correlates with my tests. I cannot find a trace of muscle weakness. As far as I am concerned, you are perfectly normal. There isn't anything wrong with you. As of now I lift all restrictions. You can do whatever you want, but do not push yourself past the point of exhaustion."

Joyce stared at him in amazement for a moment. "Praise the Lord!" she exclaimed.

Driving home that afternoon, Joyce thought of all that had happened since that night in the restaurant. No longer would she take anything for granted. She did not know what tomorrow held, but would no longer worry about it. She knew the One who knew all about what would happen the next day and the next. Her life was in His hands, and He was fulfilling His plan for her.

27

The Lighthouse Comes to the Far East

By the summer of 1985, Joyce had resumed all of her responsibilities at The Lighthouse. One beautiful morning she got up feeling as good as or better than before her battle with multiple sclerosis. Wanting to do something special that day, she decided to treat herself to lunch at the Hotel Yorktown.

As she waited for her lunch to be served, Joyce praised God for His goodness over the last several months. For some reason, Joyce's prayer partner, Kim Wicks (a blind, Korean singer), came into her mind. Joyce remembered something Kim had once said. "Joyce, God uses people who are prepared." All through lunch, those words kept coming back to her.

After lunch, Joyce stood outside the hotel wondering what to do next. Noticing the York County Courthouse next door, the thought suddenly came to her, *Why don't you go in and apply for your passport?* On a whim, Joyce followed the notion and went into the courthouse. She filled out the application and had her photograph taken.

Joyce forgot about the application until the passport arrived six weeks later. Two days afterward the phone rang.

"Joyce, this is Kim. How are you feeling lately?"

"Great!" Joyce replied, delighted to hear from her friend.

"You remember me saying to you that God uses people who are prepared?" Kim asked.

"Yes," Joyce said.

"Do you by any chance have your passport?"

"Why, yes, I do," replied a surprised Joyce. "It arrived just two days ago."

"Well," Kim said excitedly, "I am planning a trip to Korea and the Philippines in October, and I need someone to accompany me as a guide. If you will agree to go, a friend of mine will pay all of your expenses!"

"Well . . . ," Joyce hesitated, "that's great!"

"Are you willing?" Kim asked.

"Yes," Joyce said, "but I will have to discuss it with Morgan before I give you a final answer. We have five college girls living at The Lighthouse now, and I will have to make arrangements with them, too."

Joyce agreed to call Kim back as soon as possible. That night when Morgan came home from work, Joyce told him about Kim's offer. Morgan thought it was a great idea, but said it would be good to discuss it with the other household members.

When told of the trip, the five girls were delighted and agreed to plan the meals and take turns cooking and cleaning the house. Those details cared for, the decision was made. Joyce telephoned Kim the next day and relayed the good news.

On October 9, 1985, Joyce boarded a plane with Kim at Los Angeles, and the two were underway. Traveling overseas was new to Joyce, but the Lord gave her patience as they waited in lines for customs, transfers and baggage checks. Their first stop after leaving the States was in Japan, where they were to change planes for Korea. Joyce thought, *Wouldn't it be great if I could see one of my Japanese girls?* But there was no time for that.

In Korea, Kim was scheduled for several radio broadcasts with the Far East Broadcasting Company. After nearly a week here, the two traveled to the Philippines, where Kim was to take part in a three-week evangelistic crusade. During their visit here, Kim made several television tapings to be shown later in the year. On one show, the producers even asked Joyce to give testimony to her healing of mulitple sclerosis.

After nearly a month of traveling, Joyce was ready to go home. She missed The Lighthouse, Morgan and the girls. Looking out the plane window at the blue Pacific Ocean below, Joyce guessed she would never see this sight again and thanked the Lord for His goodness and this opportunity. She turned to Kim and voiced her thoughts.

"Never say never!" Kim said. "You don't know what the Lord may have in store for you in the future."

Joyce arrived home November first and spent

the next several days recovering from the dysentery she had acquired during her visit in the Philippines. Three days after arriving home, another surprizing call came. Morgan answered the phone.

"Morgan, this is Junko," the caller said. "I'm calling to ask your permission for Joyce to come to my wedding on November 25th. If she can come, I will send her a plane ticket and pay her other expenses.

"It sounds good to me. Hold on a minute," Morgan said, "I'll get Joyce on the phone."

"Junko!" Joyce exclaimed as she picked up the phone.

"Joyce, I am sending you a round-trip ticket to Japan. I want you to come to my wedding. I asked Morgan, and he said it would be OK for you to come. Will you?"

Totally surprised, Joyce looked at Morgan. "Go!" he said, smiling.

The arrangements were made, and Joyce hung up. Thoughts of Junko flooded her mind, and Joyce was on cloud nine!

On a jet over the Pacific once again, Joyce could not help but remember her trip overseas with Kim and the experience through customs. *The Lord was preparing me for this trip*, she thought to herself. As the plane approached the airport, Joyce whispered a prayer, "Father, show me what You want me to do in Japan. I feel so helpless, but I am depending on Your help and guidance. You gave me this opportunity, and I want to use it for Your glory."

Customs at the airport in Japan went quickly, and Joyce emerged expecting to be greeted by her Japanese friends, Rieko (another York College student) and Keiko. No one was waiting for her, though, and Joyce did not know what to do. Here she was, in a Japanese airport where no one spoke English, and she had no Japanese money. She could not even make a phone call. Not knowing what else to do, Joyce decided to find a seat near the airport's main entrance. *Perhaps they have been delayed for some reason*, she told herself. While sitting there—on her suitcase because she could not find another seat—she seemed to hear the Lord say to her, "I am with you always. Be still and wait."

Three hours later, the two young women came running into the airport. Spotting Joyce, they came over full of apologies. They had missed the train to the airport. Assured that Joyce was fine, the three spent a few moments in joyous reunion—the two Japanese girls calling Joyce their American mother.

They traveled to the evening's accommodations, and the next day, Joyce took a bus to Tokyo. Reverse culture shock hit as Joyce was ushered into her hotel room. A folded kimono lay on her bed and hot tea sat on the table.

That night, Joyce met Junko and her mother in the lobby. What a reunion this was! Junko was absolutely radiant as she introduced her American mother to her Japanese one. The three had dinner together, and Joyce and Junko's mother exchanged gifts.

Before Junko and her mother left, Junko asked Joyce a question. "Would you give a short speech at my reception tomorrow?"

"OK," Joyce replied, "but what would you want me to say?"

"Whatever is on your heart," Junko replied winking at her.

Joyce then knew Junko wanted her to tell something about Jesus. Saying good night to Junko and her mother, Joyce returned to her room, praising God for this answer to prayer. She now knew that God was allowing her to be a "missionary" to the Japanese people who would be at Junko's wedding.

The next day Junko's parents and other relatives met Joyce in the lobby. As they greeted, Junko's father noticed a brooch Joyce was wearing and pointed to it. Smiling, Joyce pointed at the brooch, then at him. He had sent the brooch to Joyce as a gift of appreciation for her care of Junko during her stay in America.

The first part of the wedding ceremony was for the family only, but Joyce was invited to attend. At the reception, important people in Junko's and Keeichi's lives stood to make speeches about the bride and groom. Keiko, who sat by Joyce, interpreted the testimonials. Then Joyce heard the master of ceremonies call her name. More than a little afraid, Joyce made her way to the microphone accompanied by Keiko. Under her breath, she uttered a quick prayer. "Lord, here is my opportunity. Help me to say the right things."

Joyce began by thanking Junko's parents for inviting her to the wedding. "This is a special celebration for me. I feel as if Junko were my own daughter. We called her our Japanese Princess. I wish my family in America could be here and see her today. She truly is a princess!"

"I am glad God brought Junko and Keeichi together," Joyce continued. "One symbol of this special day are the rings that were exchanged. They will be a special reminder of their love for each other. The rings are round. They have no beginning or end. You know what that reminds me of? It reminds me of God's love for Junko and Keeichi and for all of us. A very special book, the Bible, says that 'God so loved the world that he gave his one and only Son, that whoever believes in him shall not perish but have eternal life.'"

"My prayer for Junko and Keeichi is that God will be the Head of their home and that Jesus Christ, His Son, will be evident in their lives as they serve Him together. God bless you, Junko and Keeichi, now and forever."

As Joyce stepped away from the microphone, she looked at Junko. Tears of joy ran down her face. Joyce remembered how they had talked of this day and how Junko so wanted her parents and relatives to hear the good news of Jesus Christ.

After the reception, Junko's mother thanked Joyce for her words, giving Joyce assurance that they had been accepted.

While the newlyweds honeymooned, Joyce spent several days touring Japan. The highlight of the sightseeing trip was her visit to the Osaka International Church where Joyce heard the testimonies of young Japanese believers.

Back in Tokyo, Joyce was able to spend a few days with Junko before returning to the States. The two talked of Junko's trip to America and the many good times at The Lighthouse. It was a wonderful time of fellowship for both of them.

On the trip back home, Joyce could not help but think of the time when she and Morgan had said, "Yes, Lord" to His will for their lives. They had thought at the time that He might be calling them to overseas missionary service. Instead, He brought the mission field to their door. Over the years, though, Joyce had not forgotten this overseas missionary vision. Part of it had been fulfilled when God brought Orientals to The Lighthouse. Now, with the trip to Korea, the Philippines and, finally, to Japan, God had fulfilled the rest.

28

A Personal Word from Joyce

If I speak in the tongues of men and of angels, but have not love, I am only a resounding gong or a clanging cymbal. If I have the gift of prophecy and can fathom all mysteries and all knowledge, and if I have a faith that can move mountains, but have not love, I am nothing. If I give all I possess to the poor and surrender my body to the flames, but have not love, I gain nothing.

Love is patient, love is kind. It does not envy, it does not boast, it is not proud. It is not rude, it is not self-seeking, it is not easily angered, it keeps no record of wrongs. Love does not delight in evil but rejoices with truth. It always protects, always trusts, always hopes, always perseveres.

Love never fails (1 Corinthians 13:1–8a).

EACH PERSON WHO CAME into our home helped make that portion of Scripture real to me. As I look back, I can remember so many times when the verses came to my mind. I had to remember that love is patient and kind, that it hardly notices when someone does something wrong. I realized that if the individuals who came across our path were really going to see Jesus Christ in our lives, it would have to be through the way we showed them love. Nothing we did would amount to anything unless it was done with love.

Before I could practice that kind of love, though, there was something I had to do—and still have to do—daily. Matthew 16:24 states, "If anyone would come after me, he must deny himself and take up his cross and follow me."

What has it meant to me to take up my cross? Well, it has meant giving up my kitchen; not having everything perfectly clean or in the right place; sharing the washer and dryer; having no hot water left for my bath; staying up long hours of the night listening to someone pour out his or her heart; cooking extra meals when I thought I had the evening off; carrying large bags of groceries and doing extra shopping; having all kinds of phone calls and phone bills and waiting for my turn to use the phone; staying home when the rest of the family is planning a weekend trip; taking trips to the doctor's office and waiting, waiting, waiting; standing in long lines with others at the unemployment or welfare offices; being a peacemaker; keeping open lines of communication between our own children and especially between Morgan and myself; not taking our own children for granted.

Let me say that this last has been one of the hardest things to do. Often our own children would take second place because we had to spend time with our guests to deal with their urgent problems. I have this special thing with Amy and

Beth, though. I told them that if they ever felt neglected or rejected, they should come to me and say, "Mom, I need a hug." There were many times when they had to say that to me, reminding me that I needed to be sensitive to their needs. They have been so good in sharing—sharing their bedrooms, their clothes, their mother and father.

Loving also means not being able to just take off and go somewhere; putting myself last— almost all the time; giving up what I used to think was mine; and coming to the realization that when I say "Yes, Lord" to what He wants me to do, it really means "Yes, Lord."

Jesus told us in Scripture that serving Him would cost us something, and if it does not cost something, it is not worth much. Loving costs. Serving Jesus costs. It cost us in all the ways I just mentioned as well as financially, but it is worth it! I know it sounds trite, but I would not trade our experiences at The Lighthouse for any-thing in this world.

The key to keeping my sanity has been spending time alone with God, praying and reading His Word. A favorite devotional of mine has this line: "One hour of concentration gives you an hour of illumination." I cannot reflect Jesus unless I have been with Him.

It is easy to get burned out. I have experienced that, and it usually happened when I was not consistently praying and reading the Bible. The only way the ministry at The Lighthouse works is by drawing upon Jesus' strength.

Every time I go through a drought, I know the Lord is faithful. The only way to survive is through the Word. The Bible says, "I will pour water on the thirsty land, and streams on the dry ground."

When I am going through one of these times, I tell Morgan, "I am going through a desert." Then I hear the Holy Spirit's voice saying, "Hang on, I have water for you. I am going to give you a drink."

One of these drought periods came when we hit bottom financially. Many people have asked where the finances come from that keep The Lighthouse afloat. Some assistance comes in the form of private donations, but these amounts are small. Most of the money comes from my work as a private-duty nurse or from Morgan's overtime earnings. The Lord does not always provide money in miraculous gifts from heaven. Instead, He provides us with opportunities to earn additional money, and our part is to accept. At this one particular time, though, expenses far exceeded income. There seemed no way out of the predicament except to sell The Lighthouse. So we contacted a realtor and put the house on the market. It was to appear in the county multiple listings book July 1st.

A few days later, we heard a knock on our door. As we opened it, we were greeted by a man who said he was new to our neighborhood. "I can't stay," he said hurriedly, "my wife and I are going shopping, but we wanted to give you this. We have heard about your ministry here and wanted to help support it. I am giving you a check for seed faith for The Lighthouse. Use it to meet some of the needs of your home."

The check was for $111.11. On the line where the amount was written numerically, a triangle was drawn above the first three ones. This added triangle made the figures look like a house.

The gift was an encouragement to us and proof that God wanted us to stay at The Lighthouse. We immediately contacted the realtor and told him to take the house off the market.

It seems that God has a sense of humor, too, when it comes to supplying our needs. One November, some of Morgan's co-workers were on their way to a job. Driving down Interstate 83, they happened to spot a live turkey standing by the road. It had evidently escaped from a truck that was hauling turkeys to a slaughter house. The men stopped, caught the bird and stowed it in the back of the truck.

As the day's work came to a close, they still had the turkey and did not know what to do with it. One of them suddenly thought of Morgan and our situation at The Lighthouse. "Let's give it to Morgan," he said, "he can use it for his Thanksgiving bird." It just so happened that Morgan was off work sick that day. When the company truck drove up in the driveway, he did not know what to expect. Everyone laughed when they came to the door with the turkey, but it was gladly accepted and became the main course at our Thanksgiving feast!

I have also learned that the key to getting through difficult times is to simply praise Jesus! Our human reaction is to sink into depression, and I am no exception.

I could, if I let circumstances overwhelm me, easily succumb to this depression—especially when I am physically tired. I have learned, though, that when these times come, they are really times of spiritual testing. We are literally in a spiritual battle. I have to claim authority over my feelings of depression through Jesus Christ. I know ultimately that the attacks are from Satan. He does not want this house to keep going. He does not want us to experience victory, so he bombards us with all sorts of things. I have learned, though, with Jesus' help, to be persistent during these tough times. The truly amazing thing is that these times of testing always seem to come before a major victory, and it is remembering this that keeps me careful to look to Christ for that victory.

Whenever I feel overwhelmed, I know I have to get alone and begin praising Jesus for everything. God says through Isaiah, "He has sent me . . . to bestow on them . . . a garment of praise instead of the spirit of despair" (Isaiah 61:1–3). As I start praising Him, the spirit of despair instantly leaves!

Jesus has already won the victory for us. He is our reason for being, our strength to carry on. He is constantly there with us, and everything we do is for Him!

And Some Comments from Morgan

I HAVE HEARD IT said that God does not ask you to do anything that He does not equip you for first. As I look back to the first time I told the Lord I would do His will, I realize that I was not really qualified or equipped for what He wanted me to do. I do praise Him for being patient with me, though, and for allowing me to come to know Him personally.

I remember, when I was 12 years old, of daydreaming and wondering what the future might hold for me. In my neighborhood, there were some unruly boys and girls. Many of them, I knew, came out of difficult home situations. Deep down inside, I felt sorry for these children, and I remember saying then that I hoped someday I would be in a situation to help hurting people.

As I got older—and busier—I lost this concern for those in need. Through those years I missed many blessings because I was busy doing my own thing—getting married, having children, owning a house and a nice car and saving money. I remember thinking that if I could somehow accumulate enough money in the bank for the children's college education by the time they were ready to go to college, I would be a truly happy man.

Because I felt that what I had belonged to me, I had a hard time letting go of material possessions. As a result, I was never satisfied with what I had. Our house was never nice enough or big enough or furnished well enough.

But God did a work in my life. He replaced my perspectives with His own. Instead of becoming a self-made man, I found Jesus turning my life around and helping me become a God-made servant.

When Claude asked us to move to his house, these feelings of ownership still possessed me. There was a certain pride attached to moving into this nice house on Country Club Road. After Claude died, it took some work for the Lord to show me that this house belonged to Him, not to Joyce and me.

Another lesson that I learned is that everyone needs help. Claude needed help. Everyone misjudged him because he did not allow people to really know him. He would use people. If he became your friend he had a motive. He hoped to use you somewhere down the line. In our case, he was desperate. Either he would accept our help or be placed in a nursing home, which he did not want. But he also knew that we would need help—his help—in running the house.

Everyone who has lived at The Lighthouse has been part of the family. They have all had the rights any other family member would have. One of my favorite ways of making people feel at home is to tell them to feel free to raid the refrigerator.

Claude was no exception. He was not allowed to live behind the closed doors of his room. We insisted, in fact, that he had to keep his door open. The children had a right to come into his room, to share and to be a part of his world. He agreed to that. One doctor told us that the children and the family environment, not his medication, extended his life.

And Claude helped me, too! He taught me about banking, budgeting, maintenance and staying on top of things. If you have a big place, you must manage it properly. Priorities are important.

I thank God for the time my wife and I said "Yes, Lord" at a missions conference at our church. The invitation was for those who felt a call for missions, and we did feel that call. In our minds, we envisioned some faraway land we would travel to. But then He showed us that our mission field was our front door, and that He could use ordinary people right where they were for His service. He then proceeded to bring those in need to us. Doing His will meant ministering to those around us.

The ministry grew out of sharing and caring for those in need—sharing not only our home and possessions, but ourselves and God's love.

We could have kept a list of all our possessions and checked it after each person departed—especially those with criminal records—but that would not have been trusting God. God showed us that these material things were tools that could be used by Him to help others. They were not really ours anyway, but His!

The people who have lived here have enjoyed the nice things—some were Claude's, some ours. Many could not believe they were going to be sleeping in such a nice place as Claude's room. When they would come into that room, many would stand in awe of its elegance. The Lord has used that room—and the whole house—as a tool. In fact, there has been a conversion in nearly every room of the house.

At the beginning of our ministry, Jesus had to teach me patience. Even though I wanted to be a servant, I did not have patience. I now can see that by being obedient and allowing Him to carve and chisel me those first few years, he has rewarded me by seeing people's lives changed and their confession of Jesus' love.

Some of the people, when they first came, were real problems. They tried our patience. They would lie to us. Many had lied about their conversion just so we would take them in. In just a few weeks, though, those same people would come to us and apologize, confessing their wrongdoings. I could have gotten angry and told them to pack their bags and leave, but when I allowed the Lord to work in their hearts, I saw results—in their lives and my own.

God also had to teach me patience about finances. Many times, things were tight, but God always seemed to provide. As Joyce has already mentioned, needs were not usually met in miraculous ways. Most of the time, the extra money came through overtime at work or other special work opportunities. One of these was the time I helped in the Three Mile Island reactor clean-up.

I work for Metropolitan Edison Company, a utility company that services the York County area where we live. After the accident at Three Mile Island, the company asked for volunteers for the clean-up crew, particularly those who already had their families—radiation can cause sterilization. Well, we had four children and did not expect to have any others, so after praying about it, I felt I should volunteer.

Before I started, God gave me a Scripture verse as a promise of His protection: "Do not be afraid, . . . I am your shield," (Genesis 15:1). At the end of each day, we had to be tested for radioactivity. Consistently, I came up with the lowest figure. God was true to His promise.

That was not all, though. God gave me opportunity to witness to the other men on the crew. When they asked me if I was not afraid of radiation, I told them, no, that God was my shield. One young man even went to a bookstore to purchase a Bible—he wanted God as his shield, too!

Another example of God's goodness concerns my vision. After my eye operation at Johns Hopkins, I could really only see out of one eye. I feared, because of possible loss of depth perception, that I might lose my job. But God has been faithful. Never once have I experienced vision problems on the job—and I have no problem with depth perception.

God has given me opportunities to witness through this, also. When others ask me about my eyesight, I tell them that God looks out of my right eye, and I look out of my left. It has been a good partnership.

I feel our part in the ministry at The Lighthouse has been to do Jesus' will. We plant the seeds, and He waters. We try to instruct individuals in the living of a fruitful Christian life. We also try to teach them how to survive in today's world—how they can live in the world, but not be a part of it.

So I would agree with Joyce that none of what we do would be possible without Jesus Christ and His sustaining and providing hand. He lets us see people from His vantage point and gives us the love to love people who are not necessarily easy to love.

CHAPTER
30

And Some Words from Their Children

Shonna: During the first years of the ministry at The Lighthouse, I was away at college. After that, I spent time in the Army and then lived on my own. As a result, I never experienced the day-to-day life of The Lighthouse.

Later, though, I made the decision to move back home for a while. This was during the time when Dwayne, Danny and one of the Japanese girls were also living there. Daily interaction with these individuals and seeing how my parents reacted to everyday situations gave me an appreciation for what they were doing. As I told my parents when I moved out, I finally understood why they did what they did.

Although I really didn't feel part of the ministry, Mother tells me that I still played an important part. Everyone who lived there knew about me, and when I wrote home, they all shared in my parents' joy as the letter was read around the supper table. They even prayed for me during their devotions or at mealtime.

If I could say one thing about The Lighthouse ministry, it has made me aware of those in need around me.

Mark: When we opened our home to people in need, Mother and Father continually reassured me of their love. "You are our child," they would say. "These people need help, and we want to show them what a family is and how it works. But they will never take your place." Because of that, I never felt threatened. I knew I would always have my room and my parents.

There were probably times when I wished I could have spent more time with my parents, but frankly, I don't remember any of them. As an adult, I've learned that the more responsibility a person has, the less time he has. Maybe it is just one of the Lord's miracles that I can't remember or harbor any bad feelings about being "short-changed" by my parents. I do remember, though, that when I needed them, they were there.

After I accepted Christ as my Savior, I better understood why my parents did what they did. I began to see the Lord working and changing lives. Soon, I, too, wanted to share Jesus with our new family members.

One thing that stands out in my mind is the fact that my parents always made sure that we never came home to an empty house. I know it sounds like a small thing, but it was important. My father told me that he had to come home to an empty house when he was growing up, so he wanted to make sure that didn't happen to us.

The Lighthouse ministry has given me a love for large families—my wife and I already have three children! Our immediate family was large, and our extended family was even larger. As a result, I learned that there was more to life than just myself. There are so many people in the world who need help, who need Jesus. By giving them a helping hand, you make your own life better.

What impressed me the most, though, was the changed lives of the people who came to live in our home—and how they have gone out and changed the lives of people they have come in contact with.

Amy: Only after I moved away from my family did I realize that they were different from most families. I never realized that God used my parents in an unusual way. I somehow had the notion that all Christians did what my parents did.

I do know that my parents were genuine, though. They acted the same around friends, family or the pastor. I learned early, through their example, what it meant to have a relationship with Jesus Christ. Because they lived the gospel, I knew that it was something real and not just something we talked about.

Forgiveness has always been a big part of our family. We knew we weren't perfect, and we could always say that we were sorry, hug, kiss and make up.

A big part of our family's success was in being able to laugh. We had a lot of laughter, fun and special parties. We would laugh at the supper table at the funny things that happened to us during the day. It was a healthy way for us to work out our problems.

The ministry at The Lighthouse wasn't anything spectacular. It was just a way of life, of working hard to make things work out. Jesus was there, though, and He was part of every day.

I really enjoyed having people stay in our home. It enriched my life, taught me to share and helped me get to know other people. It also taught me that you can't do everything in your own strength. God has to be an integral part of the ministry.

My husband, Steve, and I feel led to overseas missionary work. Growing up in The Lighthouse gave me a burden for others, for those in need. My missionary vision is a direct result of The Lighthouse ministry.

In Psalm 44, David says, "I do not trust in my bow, my sword does not bring me victory; but you give us victory over our enemies, you put our adversaries to shame. In God we make our boast all day long, and we will praise your name forever" (verses 6–8). It was not the bow or the strength of the sword that made the victory in David's life; it was the Lord. Similarly, it was not that we were a unique family that caused the ministry to succeed. We are very ordinary people. My sister and I fought. My father came home tired and grubby at night. My mother got tired of cooking all the time.

Yes, we were a normal family, but we had God on our side. It was in His strength that the ministry succeeded—and because of Him that it existed.

Beth: Being the youngest in the family, I have been a part of The Lighthouse ministry from its beginning. When I was four, I remember Mother taking us to convalescent homes to distribute fruit to the people, to play games with them or to just offer a word of encouragement. She was a perfect example for me, showing love and hospitality and being sensitive to people in need.

I was six years old when we started taking people into our home. Because I was young, I just accepted it as something natural and tried to make the people feel at home.

That attitude has remained a part of my personality down through the years. I am sure there were times when I wished that there were fewer people or less commotion or that I could have my parents all to myself, but I survived! Overall, I am happy for the people I got to know—my brothers and sisters in the Lord.

During my elementary years, I loved the excitement of the new babies at The Lighthouse. Because I was the youngest, I would not have had the experience of a baby brother or sister. With the girls from New Life for Girls, though, I had that joy.

The Orientals that stayed with us gave me a hunger to reach out to people from other cultures. At college, I share a mailbox with a Nigerian woman, the mother of three, whose husband was murdered. We have had special times talking and sharing with each other, building a close friendship.

There were times when people younger than I stayed at our home. I learned that I had to be an example to them, and that everthing I did was observed. It was important to establish myself as a role model.

I also learned to be open. Many times, a girl

would want to borrow my clothes. That may sound like a trivial thing, but to someone living with you, it can be a crucial matter. Waiting in line for the bathroom or being asked to turn down my stereo, has taught me to be flexible and sensitive.

I praise the Lord that He has allowed me to be a part of this ministry. I know that I was an important piece of the ministry puzzle—we all were—but it was God who put the pieces together and made the whole thing work. I also realize that He used me as one of His tools by letting me be a part of someone else's life.

EPILOGUE

"Yes, Lord"

As the book goes to press, The Lighthouse, for once, is empty—a "hard" thing for Joyce to get used to. She misses most the mealtimes together—everyone sharing their day's events around the table.

"I find it awkward to cook for only two people," she says, "and a quart of milk and a loaf of bread seem to last forever! The laundry room is not in constant use, and the phone is not ringing off the hook."

But Joyce and Morgan realize that this present interlude is just another chapter in The Lighthouse ministry.

In recent years, the ministry has focused on college students, especially international ones, from York College. Joyce still has a burden for Orientals, and the Lord has given her a special vision to be a part of church planting in Japan.

Both Joyce and Morgan continue to be active in the community and with their church. Joyce is on the board of Human Life Service, a ministry that provides counseling and help to women who find themselves in a pregnancy crisis. She also serves on a task force aimed at helping pregnant teens. Both are active supporters of the Far East Broadcasting Company, holding monthly prayer meetings for the work. At The Christian and Missionary Alliance Church of York, Morgan is active in Alliance Men and Joyce, in Women's Missionary Prayer Fellowship. They both teach Sunday school. The Lord regularly opens doors for Joyce to speak to women's groups and to others about The Lighthouse ministry and what the Lord has done in her life.

One of the Psalms admonishes us to "Be still before the Lord and wait patiently for him" (37:7). Joyce and Morgan do not know what tomorrow holds, but they know the One who holds tomorrow. Their goal for The Lighthouse is the same today as at its birth—they want to put Jesus first. Their message: God can use ordinary people who love Him and who are willing to say "Yes, Lord."

ACKNOWLEDGMENTS

Special thanks to God, the Father, Jesus, His Son, and the Holy Spirit—without Them, this story would never have happened and this book would never have been written.

Also thanks to: Albert Rose, LeVinna Wilson, Dave Hake, John Curtioff, every member of the Ilgenfritz family and my many other Christian friends who have encouraged me, supported me and prayed with me through this effort.

ANTHONY J. BACHMAN

CHRISTIAN HERALD
People Making A Difference

Christian Herald is a family of dedicated, Christ-centered ministries that reaches out to deprived children in need, and to homeless men who are lost in alcoholism and drug addiction. Christian Herald also offers the finest in family and evangelical literature through its book clubs and publishes a popular, dynamic magazine for today's Christians.

Our Ministries

Family Bookshelf and **Christian Bookshelf** provide a wide selection of inspirational reading and Christian literature written by best-selling authors. All books are recommended by an Advisory Board of distinguished writers and editors.

Christian Herald magazine is contemporary, a dynamic publication that addresses the vital concerns of today's Christian. Each monthly issue contains a sharing of true personal stories written by people who have found in Christ the strength to make a difference in the world around them.

Christian Herald Children. The door of God's grace opens wide to give impoverished youngsters a breath of fresh air, away from the evils of the streets. Every summer, hundreds of youngsters are welcomed at the Christian Herald Mont Lawn Camp located in the Poconos at Bushkill, Pennsylvania. Year-round assistance is also provided, including teen programs, tutoring in reading and writing, family counseling, career guidance and college scholarship programs.

The Bowery Mission. Located in New York City, the Bowery Mission offers hope and Gospel strength to the downtrodden and homeless. Here, the men of Skid Row are fed, clothed, ministered to. Many voluntarily enter a 6-month discipleship program of spiritual guidance, nutrition therapy and Bible study.

Our Father's House. Located in rural Pennsylvania, Our Father's House is a discipleship and job training center. Alcoholics and drug addicts are given an opportunity to recover, away from the temptations of city streets.

Christian Herald ministries, founded in 1878, are supported by the voluntary contributions of individuals and by legacies and bequests. Contributions are tax deductible. Checks should be made out to Christian Herald Children, The Bowery Mission, or to Christian Herald Association.

Administrative Office: 40 Overlook Drive, Chappaqua, New York 10514
Telephone: (914) 769-9000

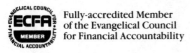

Fully-accredited Member
of the Evangelical Council
for Financial Accountability